THE PUBLIC AFFAIRS GUIDE TO SCOTLAND

Influencing Policy and Legislation

THE PUBLIC AFFAIRS GUIDE TO SCOTLAND

Influencing Policy and Legislation

Robert McGeachy and Mark Ballard

Welsh Academic Press

Published in Wales by Welsh Academic Press, an imprint of

Ashley Drake Publishing Ltd
PO Box 733
Cardiff
CF14 7ZY

www.welsh-academic-press.wales

First Edition – 2017

ISBN
978-1-86057-126-8

British Library Cataloguing-in-Publication Data.
A CIP catalogue for this book is available from the British Library.

Typeset by Replika Press Pvt Ltd, India
Printed by Akcent Media, Czech Republic
Cover photograph-Adam Elder/Scottish Parliament
Photograph © 2008 Scottish Parliamentary Corporate Body

Contents

This book is dedicated with love

from Robert to

Sandy and our wonderful children James, Eve and Olivia

and from Mark to

Heather, Adam and Lucas

Acknowledgements

We would firstly like to thank:

- Michael Clancy for his invaluable comments on early drafts of the book, and for providing the preface. Michael's success in influencing policy development and legislation at Holyrood, and at Westminster, is second to none, and we are very grateful to him for his contribution to the book.
- Mike Russell for providing the foreword to the book. His contribution to Scottish politics has been immense, and we are deeply grateful to him for his kind words.
- Ashley Drake at Welsh Academic Press for his commitment to the project, and for the highly professional and skilful ways in which he and his production team have worked with us to make it a reality. Their contribution has been exceptional.

We would also like to pay tribute to all of the Scottish Parliament staff involved in the production of the materials cited in this book. Their work in producing clear and accessible materials has made a significant contribution to raising understanding of the role of the Scottish Parliament, and of how it works. To the best of our knowledge all materials used in this book have been fully referenced. We will be happy, however, to include any references inadvertently omitted in any future editions.

We have both had the good fortune to come across a number of people who have made a major contribution in public affairs and in policy development in their respective fields, and wish to acknowledge the achievements in particular of Alex Cole-Hamilton, Kim Hartley-Kean and Maire McCormack.

And finally:

Robert would like to say a special thank you to the following people for all of their support and encouragement over the years, which is much appreciated: Jonathan and Juliet Buchan, Michael and Trish Clancy, Brian Gardiner, Ewan and Claire Cameron, Mrs Ruth Crawford, Bryan Christie, Jim Stephens, James Cameron, Cairns Leslie, Alison Kirkwood, Martin Dewar and Paul Gray.

Mark would like to say a special thank you to colleagues who have taught him so much: Mark Sydenham, Peter McColl, Sarah Beattie Smith, Richard Meade, Robin Parker, Martin Crewe, Eddie Follan, Lisa Gamble and Nicki Wray.

Robert McGeachy and Mark Ballard

Foreword

"Lobbying" said David Cameron in February 2010 "is the next big scandal waiting to happen." And happen it did, at Westminster at least, with sting activity by the media exposing the apparent willingness of some very senior political figures to offer privileged access to the corridors of power in exchange for monetary reward.

The Scottish Parliament, I hope, does things differently. 'Paid Advocacy' on behalf of any organisation is a criminal offence for MSPs – and has been since the foundation of the Parliament in 1999 – and although the big commercial lobbying companies now hover round Holyrood almost as thickly as they cluster round Westminster, most MSPs exercise understandable caution in dealing with their employees.

However, such is the difference in style and operation of lobbying on a smaller and more intimate scale north and south of the border that I almost invariably welcome and find very useful the contacts, interaction and support I have from a wide range of bodies across different sectors both in my constituency and throughout the country as a whole.

In addition, the Scottish Parliament has recently decided to legislate in order to further regulate and publicly register lobbing activity, in a proportionate and reasonable way and there is – and should be – a clear difference between commercial companies and the third sector, voluntary and professional organisations which exist to promote and protect key issues in our country and those who are involved in them.

All that work contributes to fulfilling one of the key principles of the Scottish Parliament, enshrined in the Scotland Act – that of 'power sharing'.

This guide is primarily for those third sector groups and SMEs who should – and must – interact with the Parliament in order to further that principle not least because from that principle flows the other key elements of our young Scottish democracy: accountability; openness; accessibility and participation.

'Power Sharing' implies a truth about politics that politicians are sometimes reluctant to admit, namely that neither they individually nor parties and government collectively possess all the answers and know all the solutions to the problems that confront the people and the nation.

That is particularly true in a Parliament that is small in number and in which members are having to undertake a very wide range of responsibilities including – most taxingly of all – membership of more than one subject committee.

There is no doubt that the Parliament itself and its processes are in need of reform.   Despite the excellent leadership of successive Presiding Officers and the detailed work of the members of the Bureau, the Corporate Body and the Parliament's own Standards & Procedures Committee it has become obvious that the workload even at present is too great and the pressure on committees and the chamber too intense.

The present structures were also designed for a situation in which no party would hold a majority and change to encompass such a difference is required not least in the resourcing and strengthening of the committee system.

In addition more powers are coming to the Parliament with the very modest Calman proposals now largely in effect and the Smith Commission recommendations in the last stages of coming into law.

Effective and informed activity by MSPs, the Parliament, the Scottish Government and third sector bodies in taking forward legislation and promoting causes, whilst protecting the most vulnerable is the best way to ensure a truly participatory, power sharing democracy and that is why this guide will be so useful.

Some practical examples of how beneficial such co-operation can be are given in this book, but from my own experience I would cite two interactions that were of particular importance to me.

Firstly, when in Government as Education Secretary, I was able to develop a productive and positive relationship with the National Union of Students and by engaging their representatives in working groups and on committees set up to examine particular issues – and then by giving them statutory rights to take part in bodies such as the Higher Education Forum – HE and FE funding and legislation was refined and developed to more closely meet student needs and aspirations.

That did not result in the NUS getting everything they wanted, nor did it lead to the Government doing everything right, but it did produce better outcomes than either confrontation or brief, formal discussion once or twice a year.

Secondly I would cite the work that I undertook as a member of the Rural Affairs, Climate Change and Environment Committee on the recent Land Reform Bill. I and several of my fellow members could not have participated as fully as we did, and certainly could not have moved amendments that improved the bill, if we had not been closely supported by outside bodies including – in my case – Community Land Scotland and Environment Link.

Community Land Scotland, driven forward with energy and wisdom by one of my predecessors as Education Secretary, Peter Peacock, was particularly vital in helping MSPs involved in the bill to widen their understanding of Human Rights and Land Reform across the world. With their support I organised a seminar in the Parliament on the issue which opened up new approaches and was attended by the Minister and some of her civil servants as well as by other MSPs, third sector bodies and academics.

Community Land Scotland then produced briefing papers, held meetings with committee and government officials, discussed draft amendments and helped the Clerks to the Parliament to formulate wording which had a chance of being accepted by Government lawyers; always the most exacting of judges.

After a very detailed and lengthy Stage 2, they continued to assist in helping us to achieve clarity with a definition of Human Rights on the face of the bill which resulted in a final amendment at Stage 3, which was vastly better than anything envisaged at the start of the legislative process. Moreover it will have a profound and lasting effect on land law and land utilisation in Scotland for generations to come and will underpin further much needed change.

These are only two examples – each MSP and each Minister will have many more. Children in Scotland, working in coalition with other children's charities, had a profoundly important effect on the Children's Bill in 2013/14, whilst the work of bodies supporting kinship carers has, after a long period, resulted in greater justice and support for those who take on that difficult role.

What organisations like the NUS and Community Land Scotland have done, can also be replicated with sensitivity and intelligence by any third sector body providing they know how the Government, the Parliament and the legislative system works and providing they have an open and transparent approach to dialogue.

For that is the final element that makes Holyrood very different from Westminster.

In Scotland, democracy is done in the full light of day. Soon after its establishment, the Scottish Parliament, decided to publish – in full – all the expenses claimed by its members, backed up with clear rules and procedures which ensures that members' actions and activities are fully visible and open to scrutiny. Those who work with the Scottish Parliament need to be equally open to scrutiny.

I welcome the contacts, interaction and support I have from the widest range of bodies in my constituency and across the country. Together we do a better job for all those who rely on us.

Mark Ballard and Robert McGeachy, through the pages of this important book, are therefore doing democracy a service by ensuring that best practice informs such work. I look forward to witnessing the fruits of it.

Michael Russell
MSP for Argyll & Bute
Professor in Scottish Culture & Governance,
The University of Glasgow

Preface

In living memory there has never been a more exciting time in Scottish politics. Interest in what politics is about, in activities in the Scottish Parliament and in the policies of the Scottish Government has increased steadily since the inception of devolution. The independence referendum in September 2014 energised popular engagement to an extent not experienced before in Scottish or British politics for many generations. There are many reasons for this: fluctuations in the fortunes of political parties, a desire to break the pre-existing mould of 'politics as usual', the application of technology and social media, a younger electorate and a renewed sense of the relevance of the voice of the people.

Change is in the air. Following the referendum, the Smith Commission proposed new powers for the Scottish Parliament. The United Kingdom Government then introduced a Scotland Bill to the UK Parliament. The UK Government took the view that the Bill would give effect to the Smith Commission proposals but opposition parties and others outside Parliament maintained that the Bill fell short in some crucial particulars. With the legislation now passed, the debate about the nature of the relationship between Scotland and the rest of the United Kingdom will continue and constitutional views will continue to be exchanged. No matter one's views about whether the legislation fulfilled the Smith Commission agreement, the Scotland Act 2016 contains new powers for the Scottish Parliament which will affect almost everyone living in Scotland and increase even more the focus on the Scottish Parliament and the Scottish Government. The extension of powers to include further taxation and welfare powers will affect many people and create demands on those organisations which advise them. The increased accountability of the Scottish Government will enable the Parliament to scrutinise government policies and legislation more closely and will also empower people and organisations in Scotland to question government more acutely about the decisions it makes. When these more formal aspects of political and constitutional development mix with an engaged and interested electorate which can use social media to convey their views the results will be effective in holding government to account. No longer will government only pay attention to the electorate in the run up to an election, instead a wise government will listen closely to the voice of the electorate during the whole parliamentary session. The continuous election is, in effect no longer the property of the politicians.

But political enthusiasm is not, of itself, enough. The political, legislative and public affairs agenda is complex and detailed, and is likely to become even more so with the recent vote in favour of the UK leaving the EU. This will have a significant impact on the work of the Parliament and of the Government, and on civic society in general. Apart from taxing resources, by potentially removing or restricting access to EU funding, this vote is also expected to have a significant effect on all areas in some way influenced by EU law or policy.

In order to negotiate the landscape of Scottish politics successfully and engage effectively with the governmental institutions, the political parties and the various stakeholders and sectors in Scottish civic society, any individual or organisation will need a good public affairs guide. This book is such a guide for the newcomer and a 'memory stick' for the expert. It contains all a person needs to know to engage with the Parliament, the Government, local authorities and civic society in an effective and efficient way.

The authors, Robert McGeachy and Mark Ballard, have brought together their considerable expertise in Scottish public affairs and have produced a very useful text which shines a focused light on a number of important topics. These include: the way the Scotland Act 1998 as amended works; explaining the difference between devolved and reserved powers, the Scottish Government's policy making role, the part played by Scottish Ministers, backbench and opposition MSPs, and by special advisors and the civil service. They explain how to monitor the work of the Parliament and how to work with MSPs, politicians and political parties. They cover the important issue of responding to consultations and how to inform the political and policy making agenda. This book goes into detail on the Scottish Parliament's procedures for dealing with bills and regulations and highlights the important role which committees undertake in the scrutiny of legislation and in holding Ministers to account and in initiating policy matters. The authors identify the importance of structure in campaigns to influence the law or policy making process and provide a template on how to approach parliamentary events, party conferences and working in partnership with other bodies. They also cover the important areas of working with the media and online communications; an essential aspect of public affairs work.

Politics and public affairs in Scotland is not a boring topic. This book shows how one can participate in that fast moving and interesting field and will become a tool for all who wish to get involved and to achieve success in their endeavours.

Michael P. Clancy OBE

Introduction

The Scotland Act 1998 created the Scottish Parliament and the Scottish Government,[1] and this more localised decision making has affected the lives of people living in Scotland dramatically. The UK Parliament's passing of the Scotland Act 2012 has accelerated this process by further increasing the number of policy and legislative areas over which the Scottish Government and the Scottish Parliament have control. Furthermore, notwithstanding Scotland voting to remain within the United Kingdom, the Smith Commission report[2] on further devolution of powers to the Scottish Parliament, set out a cross-party vision for further devolution through any further transfers. Some of these transfers were implemented through the Scotland Bill passed by the UK Parliament in 2016.

> Detailed information about the Scottish Parliament's 'legislative competence', and about which policy areas fall within the remit of the Scottish Parliament ('Devolved matters'), and those that remain within the remit of the UK Parliament at Westminster ('Reserved matters') can be found on the 'Devolved and reserved matters explained' section of the Scottish Parliament's website.

Since 1999 the Scottish Parliament has taken over legislative competence from Westminster on policy areas which are Devolved matters, and has passed a wide range of new laws. Some of these Acts have been very specific, such as the first Act passed in 1999 – the Mental Health (Public Safety and Appeals) (Scotland) Act – while others such as the Abolition of Feudal Tenure etc. (Scotland) Act 2000

---

1. The references in this book to the 'Scottish Government' generally means the First Minister, the Cabinet Secretaries and the Ministers known collectively as 'the Scottish Ministers'. It also includes the civil servants, and the special advisers.
2. Report of the Smith Commission for further devolution of powers to the Scottish Parliament, 27 November 2014.

and the Smoking, Health and Social Care (Scotland) Act 2005 had a much wider effect on everyone living in Scotland.

Apart from introducing legislation, Scottish Ministers[3] also have major powers to introduce policies, strategies and plans, many of which have had a significant impact upon our society. Examples include the Government's Economic Strategy,[4] its Planning Policy,[5] the Early Years Framework[6] and the Curriculum for Excellence.[7]

Various sectors have been affected by Scottish Government legislation and policy strategies and initiatives, including the private sector, the public sector and the community and voluntary sector to name but a few. It is fair to say, however, that the public affairs strategies progressed by organisations and agencies within these different sectors to influence Scottish Government policy and legislation, and the policy thinking of the Opposition parties and individual MSPs, have enjoyed mixed success since the beginning of Devolution in Scotland.

This might come as a surprise, given the Scottish Parliament's well earned reputation for openness, and its willingness to engage with different sectors, including the private sector, the public sector and the community and voluntary sector, on a wide range of issues. This openness has been gradually developed, and is reinforced by a parliamentary culture in which the overwhelming majority of MSPs have willingly complied with the Scottish Parliament's Code of Conduct for Members of the Scottish Parliament.[8] Their compliance has, to date, generally spared the Scottish Parliament the type of

---

3. The Scotland Act 1998 provides that the Scottish Executive (subsequently renamed the Scottish Government) consists of the First Minister, such Ministers as the First Minister may appoint and the Lord Advocate and the Solicitor General for Scotland. The members of the Scottish Government are known collectively as the 'Scottish Ministers', and this term is used throughout the book.
4. Scottish Government, Scotland's Economic Strategy, March 2015, Scottish Government website.
5. Scottish Government, Scottish Planning Policy, June 2014, Scottish Government website.
6. Scottish Government, The Early Years Framework, January 2009, Scottish Government website.
7. Scottish Government, A curriculum for excellence: The Curriculum Review Group, November 2004, Scottish Government website.
8. Scottish Parliament, The Code of Conduct for Members of the Scottish Parliament – Edition 6 Revision 1 (8 June 2016), Scottish Parliament's website.

scandals around sleaze which have afflicted Westminster in recent years.[9]

Organisations such as the Law Society of Scotland and the the Convention of Scottish Local Authorities (COSLA) have consistently influenced Scottish Government policy and legislation to an unprecedented extent, while other organisations in the private sector, the public sector and the community and voluntary sector have sometimes struggled to come close to those impressive standards.

In particular the performance of community and voluntary organisations in public policy and in public affairs activities has also been markedly uneven. Many organisations within this sector have engaged with MSPs up to Ministerial level on different issues, and successive Scottish Governments have generally been willing to debate these issues and to consider the merits of the cases being presented to them. In this respect, there have been some spectacular successes such as the major changes to the Children and Young People (Scotland) Act 2014 as a result of campaigning by Barnardo's Scotland, Aberlour and Who Care's Scotland, which secured the most significant changes in support for care leavers in a generation. This campaign won the Scottish Council for Voluntary Organisations' 2014 'Cracking Campaign Award'. By contrast, other community and voluntary sector public affairs strategies and campaigns have failed to deliver tangible outcomes for the organisations concerned.

For the purpose of this guide, the term 'organisation' will include private companies, public bodies and charities and community groups, as much of the advice and guidance we offer can, with careful adaption and reference to the appropriate policy and parliamentary context, be used across the different sectors.

The inability of some organisations in the private, public and

---

9. The Scottish Parliament has taken steps to introduce further safeguards through the Interests of Members of the Scottish Parliament (Amendment) legislation which received Royal Assent on 21 January 2016. The Policy Memorandum accompanying the legislation states that it includes measures to ensure that information about MSPs' financial interests is transparent and accessible. Other provisions are designed to strengthen sanctions for dealing with breaches of the rules and to make the offence of 'paid advocacy' wider; Interests of Members of the Scottish Parliament (Amendment) Bill, Policy Memorandum, Scottish Parliament's website. The Scottish Government also introduced the Lobbying (Scotland) legislation to establish a lobbying register, and a code of conduct for persons lobbying MSPs. This received Royal Assent on 14 April 2016.

community and voluntary sectors to reach their full potential in public policy and public affairs campaigns and activities can be attributed to a number of factors. These include the range, and failure to recognise the areas, of policy flexibility in which the Scottish Government, the Opposition parties, individual MSPs and local councillors will be prepared to take issues on board, and to recognise the limits of the latter's scope to make, or to secure, concessions. This difficulty also stems from a lack of clearly defined campaign aims and objectives. While for many other organisations their public affairs strategy will simply have been an 'add-on' to core business and, as such, could not be supported to a level sufficient to guarantee success. For most, however, the organisation will have failed to achieve their campaign aims and objectives, and to deliver tangible outcomes, due to a lack of expertise and experience in public policy and public affairs work.

This is not to disparage the efforts of the organisations involved, particularly because, at the time of their campaign, many of them will no doubt have been under severe pressure to keep their business or services going or, indeed for some more fundamentally, to keep their organisations afloat. Against this background, for the staff of many organisations to then be asked to launch and progress a public affairs campaign would be a daunting task, particularly if this is a new or unknown area, or if the personnel given responsibility to deliver on the strategy lack experience and expertise in this field, or do not understand the value of what they are being asked to deliver.

That said, there is no reason why an organisation cannot pursue a successful public affairs strategy which delivers all of its aims and objectives, even in the most demanding business and economic circumstances. Furthermore, it is important to recognise that organisations can develop, and deliver, a successful public affairs strategy, which does not cost the Earth.

This guide will show you what your organisation could achieve with its public affairs activities, and how to undertake these activities more successfully or better, without hiring expensive consultants or private sector lobbying companies which is often, by itself, no guarantee of success. Indeed, many MSPs, acutely aware of the Scottish Parliament's Code of Conduct, may be instinctively wary of becoming involved with such companies, regardless of their credibility and integrity. In any event, in most cases your organisation will be its own best advocate on the issues on which you are campaigning, and seeking to influence the key policy makers.

The aims of this guide are to empower organisations to undertake their own public affairs activities, and to ensure that these activities are cost effective and deliver meaningful outcomes for organisations which are often hard pressed and, as a result, struggle to engage effectively with Scottish Ministers, the Opposition parties, MSPs, local councillors and other key policymakers. It is not a detailed guide to policy and procedure in the Scottish Parliament. For those wishing such detail, it is recommended that you look at the Scottish Parliament's Guidance on Public Bills,[10] and at the Scottish Parliament's Standing Orders,[11] which set out the Scottish Parliament's procedural rules and regulations. These documents are available on the Scottish Parliament's website.

This guide will be of interest, and of use, to any organisation in the private sector, or in the public sector or in the community and voluntary sector seeking to engage with the Scottish Government, with the Opposition parties and with individual MSPs, as well as with the local government community at elected member and senior officer levels. It seeks to simplify, and to strip away the mysteries, of how organisations across the different sectors can deliver effective public affairs strategies that achieve tangible outcomes.

This guide will help your organisation to identify the relevant policy and legislative context, to adopt and develop the correct, most appropriate public affairs strategy for your organisation, and to ensure that this strategy delivers significant, meaningful outcomes for your organisation.

---

10. Scottish Parliament, Guidance on Public Bills, Session 5 Edition (Version 1, June 2016), Scottish Parliament's website.
11. Scottish Parliament, Standing Orders of the Scottish Parliament, 5th Edition (April 2016), Scottish Parliament's website.

1

Stripping Away the Mysteries

Public affairs activities

Lobbying and influencing activities can vary significantly, and can range from high profile, multi-layered campaigns which seek to influence long term change in public policy, down to the type of activities which organisations routinely take to maintain relationships with senior policy makers. The latter are often designed to raise the profile of the organisation, and to minimise the threats and risks it faces, rather than to necessarily secure significant changes in public policy.

The range of activities and initiatives involved in public affairs campaigns can be very wide and will, ultimately, depend upon the length and scale of the campaign which your organisation believes is necessary to meet its aims and objectives in the specific circumstances confronting your organisation.

However, there are some basic processes that every campaign needs to go through to be successful. Therefore this section of the guide will help you to be clear about campaign objectives, resource requirements, co-ordination and messaging.

The Seven Steps to Successful Public Affairs Planning

1 – Define what you want to achieve

This is almost always the most difficult stage, if you want to define clear outcomes rather than simply focus on outputs. While running an awareness-raising campaign may seem like an achievement, it will, however, make no difference unless the raised awareness leads to changed behaviour. The campaign is therefore an output – the alteration in reality, whether in legislation, policy or behaviour is the desired outcome.

You will need to talk this through with colleagues, teasing out exactly what it is that you want to do, and to confirm that your organisation has the *vires* to take the action in question. You need to be confident that you are clear what it is you want to do in order to get others on board.

For this reason the second part of defining what you want to achieve is ensuring you have buy-in, and ideally a firm commitment of support, from within your organisation.

Finally, you will need to be able to communicate externally what you want to do and why, in a clear and concise fashion. A good exercise is to try to summarise what you want to do in 55 words. If you cannot manage this, because what you want to do is too complex, then you probably need to rethink your activity!

2 – Support and Resources

Securing support from external partners and potential partners, and from a wide groups of stakeholders is key in terms of helping to deliver your aims.

Therefore you should ask yourself who are the stakeholders you need support from? Do you need help from others? Who are your potential allies? Who will you need on your team, both from inside and outside your organisation? As well as allies, you should also think through who you need to consult or inform about your plans. Who would be offended or upset if they did not know about your plans in advance? In this respect, it is worth bearing in mind that perceived disregard at an early stage in your strategic planning could later turn neutral observers, whether policy makers, or other organisations or influential individuals, into active opponents who could potentially derail your organisation's public affairs campaign or activities.

You also need to think about where any opposition to the public affairs activity you are about to embark on will come from. Who are the stakeholders you worry you will not get support from, and who you will therefore need to bypass or convince?

Finally, you will need to think about the resources the public affairs activity will require to succeed. Finance, staffing, space, time – how much of each of these do you think you will need?

3 – Understanding Strengths and Weaknesses

Once you have established that the project is supported and what your resource needs are, it is useful to do a SWOT[1] analysis. This will help you to consider the strengths, weaknesses, opportunities of, and threats to, your initiative, or project or campaign.

This kind of analysis will enable you to start to hone down your ideas and will give you an opportunity to look at the barriers you will need to plan to overcome, or accept. You may, for example, realise that there is a need for your organisation to research into the issue in much greater depth before you continue your planning any further.

4 – Audiences and Communication

Public affairs activities are by their very nature externally focused, but can have many audiences, or target groups. There will be decision makers you wish to communicate with, in order to persuade them to make change, and there will be those who you will want to communicate with to inspire action.

A useful exercise in developing and planning your organisation's public affairs strategy and public affairs activities is to consider your answers to the questions and issues outlined below. This will help your organisation to identify its key audiences and target groups, and to decide how best to communicate with the latter.

The problem, threat, challenge or opportunity?	
Who or what could be affected, and how?	

---

1. Although the origins of the SWOT (Strengths, Weaknesses, Opportunities, Threats) analysis are obscure, this type of analysis is widely used in business and in other sectors as a strategic planning and evaluation tool.

The person or persons responsible for the threat, who/needs to be held to account or who could create or provide the opportunity?	
The person or persons who can remove the threat, who can hold those responsible to account or who could create or provide the opportunity?	
Your proposed solution or approach?	
What outcomes are you looking for?	
The Elevator pitch - how would you tell your story to the decision maker in 50 or 60 words if you met them in an elevator?	
The key message - the memorable phrase	

You may want different messages to reach different audiences, and you may want to communicate with different groups in different ways. For each audience you need to consider what it is you are trying to communicate, and what is the best way of communicating with specific audiences. Do not forget your audiences can be very diverse with different needs, values, and access to technology – your job is to respect the various needs of those with whom you are trying to engage.

You can also think of this in terms of your short-term, medium-term and long-term targets and goals. For each of your targets and goals think about:

Who has the power to give you what you require?	
Who is able to make the decision?	
Who can directly influence those who make the decision?	

Who are the indirect influences on those who make the decisions? Who does the decision maker listen to? Will those organisations, groups or individuals support you?	

If your public affairs strategy includes a campaign you will need to make your case in a clear, concise way if that campaign is to be successful. You should be able to distil the key points of your campaign into a brief sentence and then into a short story that explains the problem and how it needs to be solved. A story that resonates with people's lives is much easier to remember than a series of technical terms and statistics, but remember not to ignore the wider context.

Use your analysis of what will appeal to your supportive influencers and supporters to prepare a convincing argument. Then turn it into a story and slogan. Good stories put a human face on the issue and often help to put the issues in perspective for the policy makers and for other key audiences, including the general public.

It is also worth thinking about the 'black holes' – the narratives that you want to avoid because they could undermine the story you are striving to tell, or which could take you off at a tangent.

5 – Developing the Strategy

Be realistic – do you have enough time, resources, people, and support for the public affairs campaign or initiative you are planning. Whatever you decide to do, it needs to be achievable – this will mean you are more likely to succeed. Vital to any public affairs campaign or initiative is the setting of objectives. You might find it useful to measure the intended effect of, for example, your campaign against a 'SMART'[2] analysis. This will also enable you to evaluate the success of your campaign. SMART analysis objectives are those that can be positively checked against the following:

- Specific: are your objectives as clear as possible?
- Measurable: how will you know how successful you have been?

---

2. As with the SWOT acronym, the origins of the SMART analysis acronym are obscure. Despite this, the SMART analysis acronym is widely used in business and in other sectors as a strategic planning and evaluation tool.

- Achievable: Are your targets achievable?
- Resourced: Do you have the resources?
- Timed: do you know what the time lines are? Have you set deadlines?

6 – Making a Plan

Effective planning is the key to success. With all public affairs campaigns or initiatives, planning is vital. Time should, therefore, be put aside to set out, and agree, a coherent set of project goals, targets and outcomes, based on what you have agreed in the previous stages.

You will need to be clear, as your plan develops, about who is responsible for each stage of the process, and the deadlines by which the latter must undertake, and complete, particular activities.

It is also vital that you are honest about the limits on your time. Good planning takes weeks, months (and even years!) rather than days. It is important to set out a timetable that includes planning and review stages, as well as your chosen activities. Evaluation should be an ongoing process – ensure you keep a record of how things are going, what comments have been made, what feedback has been received and what has, and what has not, worked throughout your public affairs campaign or initiative.

Your plan should be a timetabled set of stages to: (a) encourage the decision makers to implement your solution; and (b) encourage your potential supporters and influencers to support your organisation, and to mobilise in support of your campaign or initiative.

You also need to identify what the outcomes of your campaign or initiative are going to be, and know when you expect these to happen. Furthermore, consideration must be given to how you will measure the success of your campaign or initiative.

There are several tools you can use, one of which is action planning, to break up the campaign or initiative into stages, and to assess what needs to be done at each stage, and by whom. A template of an Action Plan is provided below.

What needs to be done?	Who is responsible?	When it must be completed?	What is needed to make it happen	Goal/outcome

What needs to be done?	Who is responsible?	When it must be completed?	What is needed to make it happen	Goal/outcome

7 – What Difference have you Made?

Continuing with the example of a public affairs campaign, as well as having a plan, it is vital that you have already thought through how you will evaluate the achievements of the campaign. It is important to not only look at the what you have done (the outputs), but also to assess the outcomes of those outputs, both intended and unintended.

Stage	Output	Intended consequences	Potential unintended consequences
1			
2			
3			
4			
5			
6			

Finally, you should look at a broader evaluation of success and failure.

Top Tip 1

Experience shows that it is not enough to be right! The history of the Scottish Parliament has seen many excellent proposals that were never acted upon because of a lack of effective public affairs work to secure support, and under developed ideas that made it into law because of excellent campaigning. The public affairs strategy should be regarded as just as important as the policy development process in securing change, rather than as an afterthought.

2

Parliamentary Monitoring

An important aspect of how your organisation can develop and progress a successful public affairs strategy, campaign or specific initiative will be ensuring it gets the policy and parliamentary context right. Accessing information about key developments at Scottish Government level, and in the Scottish Parliament, will be a vital part of that process.

Some organisations rely on subscriptions to commercial, parliamentary monitoring services, which can be expensive. However, staff in your organisation will usually always be best placed to interpret the information available at Scottish Government level, and in the Scottish Parliament, and to take strategic decisions about how your organisation can use this information to best advantage. The good news is that monitoring key business at Scottish Government level and in the Scottish Parliament is an area, which does not need to be shrouded in mystery.

With a bit of practice most organisations can update themselves about news and developments at Scottish Government level, and about key legislation, debates and questions in the Scottish Parliament. The secret is to take a more targeted approach by drawing upon the awareness of your organisation's aims and objectives, your knowledge of the sector, or sectors in which your organisation mainly operates and to identify what parliamentary business is most important for your organisation and its core business. Your organisation should then follow this business closely, and respond with appropriate public affairs activities and initiatives.

For some organisations this might not be an option due to capacity issues, while others might prefer to stick with their subscriptions to parliamentary monitoring services. In that case, pay particular attention to this chapter, and at the end consider if there are any ways in which you could get more value from the service you are currently receiving.

If, on the other hand, your organisation has some capacity, and is looking to build up its public affairs work without spending large sums of money, why not undertake your own parliamentary monitoring? With practice, this should not require too much time. Taking fifteen minutes to half an hour in the day to track key business at Scottish Government level, and in the Scottish Parliament, through their websites could identify a range of opportunities for your organisation, and identify risks and threats much earlier. It could also help to really kick start your organisation's public affairs strategy with informed governmental and parliamentary intelligence and information.

For those organisations not acquainted with the Scottish Government's website and/or the Scottish Parliament's website, and wanting to undertake your own governmental and parliamentary monitoring, you will be pleased to know that both websites are full of useful information, are accessible and are generally easy to use.

The Scottish Government's website provides an overview of the Scottish Government, its Ministers and directorates. It also provides useful information about Devolution, and about the key policy and legislative areas which are Devolved to the Scottish Parliament or Reserved to the UK Parliament. The Scottish Government's website also provides information about the Scottish Government's Concordat with the Convention of Scottish Local Authorities, and the Scottish Government's National Performance Framework, its Strategic Objectives, National Outcomes and National Indicators. In addition, the Scottish Government's website includes useful summaries of the public policy and legislative areas for which the Scottish Government is responsible.

With regard to the Scottish Parliament's website, the main section for the purpose of monitoring parliamentary business will be the Scottish Parliament's Business Bulletin. This can be found in the 'Parliamentary Business' section on the Scottish Parliament's website.

The Business Bulletin contains information about the key business in the Scottish Parliament. It is published daily (except during parliamentary recesses), and provides information about the main business in the Scottish Parliament, including parliamentary committee business, for the next week or so.

The Business Bulletin available on the Scottish Parliament's website features a Business Calendar which provides details of 'Parliament Business' and 'Committee Business' by date. Please note that there are some differences between the layout and structure of the pdf and web versions of the Business Bulletin, but that the key sections used in both are as follows:

- Today's Business
- Future Business
- Motions
- Questions
- Legislation
- More business and documents

To help you get into the habit of monitoring key business in the Scottish Parliament, you will find outlined below a short description of each section, and some advice about how you could potentially use each of these sections to the best possible effect and advantage in your public affairs strategy:

Section	Purpose	Potential use
Today's Business: Parliament Business and Committee Business	Sets out the day's business in the Scottish Parliament including legislation, debates, Scottish Government business (Motions, Statements etc.), committee business, Parliamentary Bureau Motions, Oral Questions, Members' business (usually debates)	If your organisation has already developed its own parliamentary monitoring processes, there should be no unwelcome surprises in the 'Today's Business' section. You will already have picked up the key business by looking at the 'Future Business' section, in previous Business Bulletins and as a result will already be undertaking appropriate public affairs activities in response, such as briefing MSPs before relevant debates. In this respect, you would normally only be referring to the 'Today's Business' section to double check the order of business, and timings, and also to see if any Scottish Government statements have been added to the business for that day. By contrast, if your organisation is new to monitoring parliamentary business, then try and keep a particular eye on the 'Future Business' section to make sure that you know what business

Section	Purpose	Potential use
		is coming up and have, as a result, been able, for example, to engage with the Scottish Ministers and MSPs before any relevant debates.
Future Business: Parliament Business	Sets out the future business in the Scottish Parliament, including legislation, debates, Scottish Government Business, Members' Business including debates, Business Motions, and Parliamentary Bureau Motions. This section also features details of oral questions for General Question Time, for First Minister's Question Time and for Portfolio Question Time.	Keeping an eye on this section will help you to identify key business relevant to your organisation and its work, and to identify opportunities for undertaking appropriate public affairs activities in response. Sometimes this section will lack significant details relevant to your organisation's work, which will make it difficult for you to respond quickly, and to brief the Scottish Ministers and MSPs effectively. For example notification of a debate might only become available on the Friday when the debate is the following Wednesday. This will not give you much time to prepare a briefing for MSPs, and to brief Scottish Government Ministers and MSPs. Furthermore, the wording of the motion for the debate might only become available on the Friday for a debate the following Wednesday. To give your organisation as much notice as possible to respond to key business relevant to your work, apart from checking the Business Bulletin daily, it is recommended that you also develop your contacts amongst the MSPs and their staff. You should offer to brief the MSPs for any business relevant to your organisation if they let you know in advance what is coming up. This 'belt and braces' approach will hopefully minimise the risks of your organisation getting caught out, and of being unable to brief MSPs on time about key business in the Scottish Parliament impacting upon your organisation. Having a bank of pre-existing briefing papers about your organisation, and

Section	Purpose	Potential use
		about specific issues, is another good way of ensuring that these risks are minimised. After all, if you have a briefing already on the 'shelf' you can use the Friday, when the debate is confirmed, to circulate the briefing to the relevant Minister, to key MSPs and parliamentary staff, rather than having to spend the day drafting something from scratch, and then frantically circulating it to MSPs. The latter are often inundated with briefings, so you really need to contact them as early as possible if they are going to be able to take on board your briefing, to reference your organisation during the parliamentary proceedings and to raise issues on your behalf. Developing and maintaining e-mail contact lists of MSPs will help your organisation to get its briefing for debates out quickly to MSPs. 　　You will also be able to get some advance notification of the motion for a debate by keeping a close eye on the 'Motions' section of the Business Bulletin. This includes Scottish Government Business Motions for approval, which provides a bit more detail about the forthcoming business.
Future Business: Committee Business	Outlines details of meetings and proposed future business of committees, including their agendas	This section, along with the home pages for the individual committees, will provide invaluable information about the legislation and inquiries being dealt with by each committee. Your organisation will be able to use these sources to identify opportunities to engage with the committees on relevant issues and work. This section, and the committees' home pages, will enable you to track key business relevant to your organisation's aims and objectives. 　　Check to see what opportunities there are to give oral and written evidence for individual committees' Stage 1

Section	Purpose	Potential use
		consideration of legislation relevant to your work.
		You should also use these sources to assess what opportunities there are to give oral and written evidence to individual committees for any relevant inquiries they are holding.
		Stages 1 and 2 of legislation in the Scottish Parliament are generally dealt with by the committees, and using this section, and the committee's home page, will enable your organisation to stay up to speed, and to brief MSPs at different stages of the legislation.
Questions: Oral Questions	Confirms oral questions for General Question Time, for First Minister's Question Time, for the Topical Question Time and for Portfolio Question Time	Why not approach your local MSP, or a Regional List MSP, or another MSP supportive of your organisation's work, and ask them to lodge an oral question on your behalf?
		This will give you a high profile opportunity to raise an issue/concern in the Scottish Parliament. The First Minister or another Scottish Government Minister will respond to the question, and this will present media opportunities, including using social media, to highlight your organisation's issues/concerns.
		Persuading an MSP to ask an oral question on your behalf is an excellent way of raising the profile of issues, and of using the government's response to assist your public affairs campaign or initiative.
Questions: Written Questions	Outlines questions lodged for written answer	Why not approach your local MSP, or a Regional List MSP, or another MSP supportive of your organisation's work, and ask them to lodge a written question on your behalf?
		Written questions can help to obtain vital information from the Scottish Government, which could add to the evidence base of the public affairs campaign or initiative you are undertaking.

Section	Purpose	Potential use
		A written question could also help your organisation to highlight an issue/concern, and you should work with the sponsoring MSP to investigate the potential of getting some media profile, including using social media, for the issue/concern you are raising. Such initiatives have been found to be highly effective.
Motions	Outlines all motions, and amendments to motions, lodged by the Scottish Government, and by MSPs	The Scottish Government Business Motions in this section will give you some early notice of the business which is being proposed (but has still to be agreed). It would be advisable to follow up with your MSP contacts to get some advance confirmation of when the proposed business is likely to be taken.
		This section also features motions which have been lodged by MSPs. These can be on any subject, and a brief look at this section will give you an indication of just how wide-ranging these motions can be. The 'Motions' section also includes confirmation of which MSPs have added their names to support which motions.
		A small number of the motions which are lodged lead to members' debates at the end of daily business in the Scottish Parliament.
		Most motions, however, are simply lodged to draw attention to a particular issue or to an organisation's key anniversary or to its work or achievements. These are often lodged by MSPs keen to highlight an issue or the work or achievements of an organisation/institution/individual within their constituency.
		If an MSP does agree to lodge a motion on your behalf you should liaise with their staff to see what media opportunities, including through social media, might be available to highlight the motion because, unless the motion is

Section	Purpose	Potential use
		likely to lead to a members' debate, that will be the most tangible outcome of the motion being lodged.
		Once an MSP has lodged a motion on your behalf highlighting an issue you are campaigning on or the best practice/ achievements of your organisation and its services it is advised that you phone round MSPs to encourage them to sign up in support of the motion. The sponsoring MSP will usually encourage other MSPs to support the motion, but supporting their efforts by contacting MSPs' offices will help to maximise the number of MSPs who sign up to support the motion.
		Phoning MSPs will also provide your organisation with opportunities to build up/strengthen your contacts with MSPs and their staff, as well as helping your organisation to increase its knowledge of information about the type of issues and policy areas individual MSPs are most interested in.
Legislation	Outlines progress of Bills and subordinate legislation. Also sets out new Bills introduced, new amendments to Bills and proposals for Members' Bills	This section will enable your organisation to keep itself up to speed on the progress of Bills and subordinate legislation. Other important sources for this information include contacting the clerks to the relevant committee, or visiting the relevant committee's home page on the Scottish Parliament's website or using your organisation's MSP contacts.
		If an MSP has lodged an amendment to a Bill on your behalf at Stages 2 or 3 of the legislation, this is the section you should check to make sure it has been lodged. Checking this section will also give you a sense of which other amendments have been lodged to the Bill, and which areas of the Bill are attracting the most attention from MSPs, and from other organisations.

Section	Purpose	Potential use
		The 'Bills' section also provides details of proposals for Members' Bills. In addition, this section will give you an indication of what issues are being raised by MSPs in Members' Bills, and help you to identify or finalise your own themes and issues for potential Members' Bills.
		Only a very small number of Members' Bills receive parliamentary time in which to be progressed. Most are used to raise the profile of issues, and if you do decide to work with a MSP on a Member's Bill you should liaise with their staff to consider suitable media opportunities. This is an area which would strongly lend itself to a social media campaign, which, in turn, could be used to widen support for the Member's Bill. This section should also be used to keep an eye out for the introduction of new subordinate legislation, and for the progress of existing subordinate legislation. This legislation, by its very nature, rarely receives much prominence, but nevertheless often contains very important provisions. It is generally a real challenge for most sectors trying to keep abreast of Scottish Government Bills, let alone having to worry about where to access relevant subordinate legislation. This section will help your organisation to keep up-to-date with new subordinate legislation introduced in the Scottish Parliament.
More	Provides details of additional business and documentation, including petitions lodged, new documents and corrections	This section provides information about the numerous petitions submitted by organisations and by members of the public to the Scottish Parliament's Public Petitions Committee. The 'More' section will give you a good insight into the type of issues being raised with the committee, and help your organisation to

Section	Purpose	Potential use
		identify issues on which it might want to submit a petition. Details of new documents published by, or laid before, the Scottish Parliament are featured in this section. This includes Committee Reports which are also usually featured on the Scottish Parliament's home page upon publication, The 'More' section also confirms corrections to parliamentary documents, and in particular corrections to the Official Report. It is always worth a look at this section just in case it relates to business in which your organisation has an interest.

It is hoped that this chapter will have given you an insight into how easy parliamentary monitoring can be once you strip away some of the misconceptions and mysteries which often surround it. Taking responsibility for gathering your own parliamentary intelligence could, ultimately, save your organisation significant amounts of staff time and money. It will also help to ensure that you are not missing out on opportunities which could bring significant benefits to your organisation. Keeping on top of monitoring governmental and parliamentary business will also help you to identify early any risks or threats to your organisation's reputation and to its core business.

Some final thoughts – to ensure that your organisation makes the most of its parliamentary monitoring, it is important that the parliamentary monitoring is undertaken by someone with a strong grasp of your organisation's strategic aims and objectives, its business, the sector in which it operates and its geographical spheres of operation and influence. Alternatively, the person undertaking the monitoring should be line managed, or provided with clear guidance, by a person in your organisation able to exercise such a strategic overview. Furthermore, the person with responsibility for parliamentary monitoring should ideally report their findings to a person able to exercise such an overview, and who is able to sift and interpret the information to ensure that your organisation responds effectively and strategically.

The nature of that guidance would depend upon the type of

organisation you work for. A community and voluntary organisation such as, for example, a national children's charity, operating services across Scotland, would be particularly interested in any references to children and itself or to other children's charities, to the policy areas on which it focuses and to any Scottish Government policy initiatives or funding developments relating to these areas and to the sector as a whole. It would also be interested in any references to children's services within the local authorities in which it operates, or in references to other agencies which may purchase its services such as NHS health boards.

Private companies, on the other hand, might require the monitoring of all references to the company and to its competitors, and to the industry and sector or sectors in which it operates. Companies may also have an interest in general policy areas such as planning. Their interest in more specific policy areas would depend upon the type of business they are involved in, and the sector or sectors in which they operate. Many companies will also have to keep an eye on Westminster, given the Reserved nature of some of the key policy areas relevant to their business, such as health and safety, business regulation and trading standards.

Top Tip 2
Investing even a little time on parliamentary monitoring will pay significant dividends. It will help your organisation to maximise its public affairs opportunities, and the benefits arising to your organisation from such opportunities. It could also enable your organisation to identify any potential threats and risks, much earlier and to, therefore, avoid or minimise the risks of reputational damage.

3

Engaging with Key Policy Makers

Once your organisation has identified the aims and objectives of its public affairs strategy, and the issues and/or concerns you wish your public affairs strategy or campaign or initiative to focus on, you need to consider the key policy makers whom you wish to engage with. Your organisation also needs to identify the outcomes you hope to achieve through this engagement.

Significant ways of progressing this engagement include seeking meetings with the First Minister, with Scottish Government Cabinet Secretaries or Ministers, with the Opposition parties and with individual MSPs, and also developing a programme of visits to your business, or projects or services by Scottish Cabinet Secretaries or Ministers, Opposition party spokespersons, MSPs and by other senior policy makers, including council leaders, spokespersons and key officials. Many of the principles involved in arranging such meetings/visits will be the same for a wide range of organisations.

Meetings

Before seeking a meeting with a Scottish Minister, or Opposition spokesperson, or MSP, or a Council Leader, Spokesperson or senior officer, your organisation should carefully consider the purpose of the meeting, and what outcomes it is hoping to achieve through the meeting.

Is your organisation simply seeking an opportunity to update the Minister or the Opposition spokesperson or your local MSP or council about your organisation and its work? Or does your organisation have more specific issues or concerns it wishes to raise? If your organisation is seeking to raise certain issues and concerns you will need to pay particular attention to ensuring that the arguments you will rely on are as persuasive as possible, and are backed up by robust evidence and best practice.

Take the time to think through what the politician wants from the meeting, not just what you want. How do you want them to feel after the meeting, and what are the key points that you would like the politician to remember and action? What seems important to you may not actually be a major issue for them, so focus on what they want, and you will get a better reception.

Once your organisation has addressed these factors, its main options will be to contact:

* the First Minister (although this is often extremely challenging given the competition for time in their diary);
* Scottish Cabinet Secretaries or Ministers with policy portfolios relevant to your organisation and to its work;
* senior civil servants;
* the Opposition parties' leaders;
* the Opposition parties' spokespersons on policy areas relevant to your work;
* relevant MSPs; and
* local council leaders and key spokespersons

Although the UK Parliament is outwith the scope of this guide, we would still advise you to consider adding the UK Government's Secretary of State for Scotland to the above list of key policy makers whom should be targeted, given their strategic interface with the Scottish Government. Seeking a meeting with the Secretary of State for Scotland would definitely be an option for your organisation if its focus includes policy areas reserved to the UK Parliament under the Scotland Act 1998 and the related legislation. These areas would include, for example, issues relating to asylum and immigration, employment, company law and business regulation, trade and industry, many aspects of the tax and benefits system, nuclear energy, oil, coal, gas and electricity and issues around disability discrimination. Alternatively, your organisation might, in any event, have strategic reasons for wanting to meet the Secretary of State for Scotland to share your best practice, and experience, in a UK forum.

All of the politicians on the above list are senior political figures, and extremely busy. This, however, should not put your organisation off from making such an approach. The secret is to make your request as attractive as possible to the politician and to their advisers. The chances of your organisation receiving a positive response will depend upon a number of factors, including how well your organisation presents its case, and the politician's policy and strategic priorities at the time of your approach. Other highly variable factors might also come into play, such as the proximity of elections and by-elections, the content of recent government announcements and statements, and the correlated importance of developments within the constituency/constituencies in which your organisation is based.

It is hard to be scientific about the likelihood of the First Minister agreeing to meet representatives from your organisation in response to your invitation. However, you would usually have to make an extremely strong case for this to be considered a priority for their time by their staff. A lot will depend upon the policy areas relevant to your organisation's work, and the extent to which your approach to the First Minister strikes a chord with the Scottish Government's strategic priorities, and areas of interest, at the time of receiving your invite letter.

If the First Minister is unable to meet your organisation due to their many other commitments, they might decide to pass your invite on to another member of their Cabinet, and ask the relevant Cabinet Secretary to meet you. This would still be an excellent outcome because it would give your organisation a significant opportunity to update the Scottish Ministers about your work, and to raise any specific issues or concerns.

When an organisation decides to make an approach to the Scottish Ministers it needs to make its 'pitch' for a meeting/Ministerial visit as persuasive as possible. Suggesting some policy innovations or other ground breaking initiative for the Minister's consideration, and linking your organisation's work to the Scottish Government's own policy aims and objectives, could help in this respect.

Your organisation also needs to ensure that it targets the Scottish Ministers with the lead responsibility for the areas in which you work, as well as their special advisers (details of whom can be found on the Scottish Government's website). Before sending your letter (you can phone but your organisation will usually then still be asked to put its proposal in writing) it is always worth checking with the Scottish

Government that you are writing to the correct Minister, and whether or not the policy issues you are raising fall within the remit of the Minister you wish to contact. This is particularly important where a Cabinet Secretary has Ministers in their team, and the policy areas have been divided up between the different Ministers. Getting this information right at the beginning will save your organisation time. It will also demonstrate that your approach to the Minister has been carefully considered and planned.

It is also wise not to focus solely on the party or parties that constitute the Government. You cannot afford to neglect the other political parties in the Scottish Parliament. On the contrary, it is imperative that you should always take a cross-party approach to your public affairs strategy, and are not perceived to be too closely aligned with any one political party. To ensure that your public affairs strategy is successful, and delivers tangible outcomes, you need to make your arguments and evidence as persuasive as possible to MSPs of all parties, as well as to any who are not aligned with any party and sit as Independents.

Part of this process could involve seeking support from other organisations for your strategy, campaign or initiative, and also building up a cross-party alliance within the Scottish Parliament on the issues your organisation is seeking to raise with key policy makers. This is the best way of trying to persuade the Scottish Government of the merits of your case, and of securing support from Scottish Government backbenchers within the committees for any amendments to legislation lodged on your behalf by Opposition MSPs. It is often the case that organisations' best chances of helping to shape and influence public policy and legislation is likely to lie in constructing a cross-party, and cross-organisational (and possibly cross-sectoral) alliance. Against this background, it is essential that you build up good ties and relationships with all of the parties, and with all MSPs, and you need to make sure that a key part of your public affairs strategy includes seeking regular meetings with the leaders and key spokespersons from the Opposition parties.

Making local connections work

The type of organisation you work for, and its aims and objectives, will be other important factors in determining which policy makers you should engage with. You should also be mindful of the arrangements that exist between central and local government, and how this impacts upon your organisation in terms of, for example, funding and/or your organisation's profile with Scottish Ministers, civil servants the Opposition parties, MSPs and local authorities. Whether or not it is central or local government which controls the policy levers which are of most relevance to your organisation's work, or in particular areas of interest to your organisation, is another important consideration.

Businesses, for example, might have specific concerns around issues such as planning processes and business regulation, which may necessitate approaches to both central and local government. Engaging with Scottish Ministers, civil servants MSPs and other key policy makers can also offer businesses significant opportunities to raise their profile, and to potentially capture new business or investment especially if such engagement is supported by media activities, including social media.

By contrast, funding will often be a major preoccupation for community and voluntary organisations. Under the current arrangements there is very little ring fenced funding distributed centrally by the Scottish Government, which distributes monies to the local authorities through a block grant. The local authorities, in turn, control and decide what these monies should be spent on, and how they will meet the National Outcomes and National Indicators outlined in each local authority's Single Outcome Agreement agreed with the Scottish Government.

If your organisation delivers services on behalf of a local authority or local authorities, and your public affairs strategy is about raising your organisation's profile, generally but primarily, to secure existing business and/or to potentially win new business, then you need to focus first and foremost on ensuring that your local authority or local authorities' funders, and key officers and councillors, are firm supporters of your organisation and its work. Their support and appreciation will be vital when it comes to the local authority setting budgets, and to the hardnosed discussions that take place within local authorities about which organisations will receive funding, and at what level.

If your organisation's projects and services are local authority funded, or you work in close partnership with local authorities or with a specific local authority, you need to ensure that you keep your local authority partners fully informed and involved in the planning of any visits by Ministers and MSPs. You need to be aware that council elected members will often want, for political reasons, to be involved in any such visits, and you have to ensure that strategically you are giving them their 'place'. This would be particularly true in relation to inviting council leaders, and councillors with lead responsibility for the areas you are working in, to attend an event to celebrate a key landmark development or anniversary at one of your projects, and which will involve a Scottish Cabinet Secretary or Minister or local MSP giving the keynote speech. The councillors might expect to have a formal role in the programme you plan for the visit. It is strongly advised that organisations should be particularly sensitive to partners' feelings where the visiting Scottish Minister or local MSP is of a different political party from the party running the council. If you lose sight of this dynamic, failing to involve the relevant local councillors could create tensions and cause embarrassment for your organisation, and you should work with partners to ensure that tensions are minimised, and that the visit is a great success and a positive experience for all concerned.

Arranging regular meetings with councillors with an interest in your organisation's work can potentially be very productive, particularly if your organisation closely aligns any visits to its projects/services with media opportunities, including social media coverage. It is strongly recommended that your activities in this area include meetings with the council lead spokespersons for the policy and service areas covered by your organisation's work. For businesses or community and voluntary organisations delivering services on behalf of local authorities it is also essential that you keep senior officers on board, and fully up to speed with your work (strategically, it will be beneficial to extend this beyond any normal, contractual reporting requirements you may have with the local authorities).

Ministerial visits and meetings

Having engaged with key local councillors, you should also try and engage with Scottish Ministers, Opposition spokespersons and with MSPs to raise the profile of your business/projects/services. This can be done by developing a programme of visits by Scottish Government Ministers and civil servants, Opposition spokespersons and MSPs to your business/projects. These visits can potentially offer significant benefits to your organisation. They offer major media and profiling opportunities, including social media coverage, which you can identify and progress with the Minister's media team or with the Opposition parties' spokespersons or MSP's office.

The importance of such visits cannot be underestimated – they could literally be the difference between life and death for your organisation, or for one of your businesses/services/projects. A Ministerial visit focusing on the invaluable work your organisation is doing, and its significant contribution to local communities, will offer a powerful message to your partners, sponsors, funders etc. Ministerial endorsement could, for example, have a positive bearing in any challenging discussions with your partners and funders around future funding or new contracts or extensions to existing contracts, particularly if the Minister and the council are from the same political party. Such visits will also offer your organisation opportunities to develop new, or strengthen existing, relationships with Scottish Ministers and civil servants. It could, for example, open up your access to Scottish Government funding for research, or lead to your organisation being represented on a high level Scottish Government working group in an area central to your work.

One of the first tasks your organisation will need to address is the purpose of the meeting or of the visit. Is there, for example, a specific reason for the meeting or visit? Is it to highlight key issues/concerns, or to secure Ministerial support for your organisation and its work for the tough times ahead? Or is the purpose of the meeting or visit more generally to raise the profile of your work and of your business/services?

You also need to consider if there is a specific 'hook' which you can use to make sure the invite is pitched as attractively as possible to the Minister. Is your business, for example, expanding its operation or your organisation launching a new project/service? Alternatively, is your organisation relocating to new premises, which you want the Minister to formally open? Or is your organisation or one of its projects/services celebrating a key anniversary or landmark? Or is there a major achievement which you want to celebrate? These are just some of the hooks you could use if you want to have a 'celebratory event' involving partners, funders, staff and any service users. Such events are ideal if you want to make the most of any national and local media opportunities, and to raise the profile of your organisation and its work. This type of event would also offer good opportunities for your organisation to raise its profile through the use of social media.

As before, try to consider the invite from the politicians' point of view. What are they looking for? It could be good publicity, a chance to understand the local aspects of an issue that is coming before Parliament, or even a chance to highlight a concern about a wider local or national issue. Be sensitive to the political impact of a visit – who must attend to ensure the visit is a strategic success? Who might be upset by not being invited?

Alternatively, you could just invite the Minister to visit your organisation or one of its businesses/projects/services to brief them about your work, and to raise any issues or concerns.

The First Minister and other Scottish Government Ministers have significant workloads, and unless your organisation has already been given a strong indication (or official confirmation) that they are keen to meet representatives from your business/organisation or to visit its projects/services, you should allow at least two or three months from the letter of invite being sent to the date of the proposed Ministerial visit itself. Where you have been given such an indication/received official confirmation, then the arrangements can be finalised fairly quickly by liaising with the relevant Ministerial diary secretary. You will, however, usually still need to send a formal invite letter requesting a meeting or inviting the Minister to visit your organisation's project/ service. This is vital because different teams of officials are often involved in planning visits, and you risk the disappointment of a Ministerial double booking if you do not have a formal invite letter in the Scottish Government's correspondence system. Please be very aware that it has been known for strong Ministerial signals expressing keenness to participate in the launch of a new service to come unstuck relatively late in the day when it was discovered that a formal, written invite had not been sent and, as a result, the officials had committed the Minister to another event. We would recommend that you avoid taking any chances, and get your invite letter off early, and as soon as your organisation has agreed internally on the purpose of the meeting/ visit and on the logistics involved.

And now for a couple of other bits of advice that apply generally to all such invites, and which your organisation will find useful. Make sure that you send the letter to the correct Ministerial address, and not to the Minister's Scottish Parliament or constituency addresses.

Please also ensure that the letter is sent in the name of your chief executive, chair or senior officer, as this will have a direct bearing on the type of response your organisation receives. We would also advise you to suggest two or three dates for the visit or meeting, as this will make it easier for the Scottish Government's correspondence section, the Ministerial diary secretary and senior officials to take a view on whether or not the Minister should agree to the visit or meeting. In our experience, organisations which just send a general invite, without suggesting specific dates, are more likely to have their invites declined.

These little tips, although perhaps appearing self-evident, are not always followed, and failure to follow them will increase the risks of your organisation's invite being declined, or not being received by the officials who will be making the final decision with the Minister about which invites should receive a positive response or a polite decline.

MSP visits and meetings

MSPs are also very busy, and it is recommended that your organisation gives careful thought to how it approaches an MSP to request they visit your organisation, or to secure their agreement to meet representatives from your organisation.

Your organisation also needs to consider which MSP or MSPs it should approach. In terms of best practice, and to avoid your organisation falling foul of parliamentary protocol, we would advise you to approach your constituency MSP first. Who this is will depend upon whether or not you are inviting the MSP to visit your HQ, or to visit a local business, or project or service. From experience, you would need to have a very good reason for inviting an MSP to visit one of your businesses or projects or services and to give a speech within a constituency which is not their own constituency, or to invite an MSP from another electoral Region to make the speech. Potential reasons might be the MSP has strong links with your organisation, is the convenor of a Scottish Parliamentary Committee which is undertaking an inquiry in which your organisation has a strong interest or it is an MSP who is campaigning on a particular issue in which you are interested. If you decide to go down that route, it is strongly advised that your organisation ensures that the visiting MSP first informs the constituency MSP that they are visiting to avoid your organisation getting involved in any political 'fall-out' between the two MSPs.

If your organisation is proposing to hold a celebratory event to celebrate, for example, the 10th anniversary of a local business or project or service, and the local, constituency MSP is unable to attend, you should ask one of the Regional List MSPs to visit. If you are unsure who the local constituency MSP, and the Regional List MSPs are for your region, you can find out by undertaking a postcode search on the Scottish Parliament's homepage. By entering the postcode of your project/service this search facility will provide you with this information.

In terms of which Regional List MSP you invite as an alternative should the constituency MSP be unavailable, the constituency MSP's office might want to nominate a substitute from one of their party's Regional List MSPs. If that does not prove practical or appropriate, you should approach the Regional List MSP who strategically offers the best 'fit' with your organisation and its work.

If this happens, it is recommended that your organisation attempts to ensure that the Regional List MSP informs the constituency MSP they will be attending an event in the latter's constituency. The same consideration would apply if a list MSP contacts your organisation with a view to visiting one of your projects/services. In this context, the list MSP should let the local constituency MSP know that they will be visiting to avoid your organisation running the risks of receiving an awkward phone call from your enraged local MSP. It is recommended that your organisation bears these factors in mind with such invites, because if you get it wrong the risk is that this will have an adverse impact upon your organisation's relationship with your local MSP and their party. Strategically this could prove costly in the long run for your organisation.

One general consideration your organisation should bear in mind when inviting an MSP to one of your businesses or projects or services, is that you are more likely to be able to persuade an MSP to visit your organisation or one of its businesses or projects or services on a Friday as this is generally a non-sitting day in the Scottish Parliament. We would advise you to phone the MSP's office, and speak to a member of their staff to give them some background information about your organisation's work, and about the purpose of the invite.

If you succeed in making the case for the MSP to visit (or even if you do not) you will probably then be asked to send a formal letter of invite. This letter should say a bit about your organisation, its work and why you want to meet the MSP, or for the MSP to visit a particular project or service. You should also mention whom you have spoken to in the MSP's office, and refer to any provisional date for the MSP's visit you have identified with the member of the MSP's staff.

Planning a Ministerial or MSP visit

It is vital that your organisation makes the most of the opportunities presented by a Ministerial visit or an MSP visit to one of your businesses or projects or services. These visits are likely to play a significant role in your organisation's public affairs strategy. We would, therefore, strongly advise that you standardise your internal procedures for progressing invites to Ministers or MSPs to visit your business or projects or services or to take part in a celebratory event at your business or at one of your projects/services, and for arranging such events. Standardising your approaches to such visits/events will help to ensure that the visits/events are highly successful and productive, and attract significant levels of media coverage, including social media. It will also help to ensure that your organisation builds up significant expertise and capacity in organising such visits/events, which will make it easier and easier to organise these visits/events going forward.

Your organisation might want to use/adapt the checklist below of key tasks to progress for an invite to a Scottish Cabinet Secretary or Minister to give a keynote speech at an event to launch a new local project or service, or at a celebratory event at a business or project or service. The list of tasks is not exhaustive, but it will at least give you an indication of the type of arrangements and details you will need to progress to ensure the event is successful. This list would, with appropriate modifications, have equal application for a private company, or a public body or a community and voluntary organisation.

Who is given lead responsibility within your organisation for each of the key tasks outlined below will depend upon how your organisation is structured, and where the capacity/experience/expertise lies within the organisation for each of these particular tasks. We would also advise that you highlight the relevant deadline for each specific task, and date when achieved, and that such a template is updated daily in the run up to the visit/event.

Key Tasks and Activities to be Completed for a Ministerial Visit

Key task	Person/Team responsible	Deadline/When achieved
Preliminary arrangements		
• Agree nature and purpose of event/ visit; • Agree lead manager responsible for the event/visit, and confirm who will be in the event/visit management team; and • Ensure timeline is in place to support appropriate planning [e.g. Dates must suit diaries of key speakers and guests and key lead officers within your organisation, as well as fitting with routines of the project and any service users, partner organisations, key clients etc. as appropriate].		
Set up short life, internal project management group to organise, and to progress arrangement for, the visit.		
Agree on the desired outcome of the visit, and how you will assess whether the outcome has been achieved. Success criteria need to be more than just a successful visit – agree how you might evaluate the successful impact of the event in six months' or a year's time.		
Invite to Minister to give keynote speech to launch a new project/service		
1. Send formal invite to the relevant Scottish Government Minister.		You should allow 2–3 months from the point of the invite letter to the proposed date of the event
Taking a partnership approach		
2. Your organisation should consider how you involve partners in the event,		

Key task	Person/Team responsible	Deadline/When achieved

and what formal role they should have (if any).
    Also need to agree how partners will be represented at the event, and to get their input for the guest list as appropriate.
    Invite letter/invitations should be prepared by your organisation's staff, and be approved and signed off by the Chief Executive/lead officer.		

Other guests		
3. Prepare guest list. This is an important opportunity for your organisation to maximise the strategic impact of the event by making sure that all of the key people you wish to influence attend.		
Programme		
4. Prepare programme for event. Send programme to the Minister's office (or to the MSP's office as appropriate) for comment Send out invitations/invitation letter and, as appropriate, the programme to guests.		
Administrative arrangements for the event		
5. Project/service staff to monitor confirmations of those attending, and to keep senior management updated on overall number of attendees.		
6. Need to maintain good liaison with key partners about the arrangements for the event. To help this process, a list of key contact details should be prepared. Key partners for visits by Scottish Ministers (or as appropriate for a visit by an MSP) would include, for example: • Scottish Government – Cabinet Secretaries or Minister's office and officials;		

Key task	Person/Team responsible	Deadline/When achieved
• MSPs (Constituency and Regional List); • Local authorities (elected members and senior officers); • Funders; • The private sector; • Public bodies and other agencies; • Community and voluntary sector organisations You also need to consider who should attend from your own organisation, e.g. the Chief Executive, senior managers, trustees, directors, business partners, customers, existing and previous service users.		
Publicity		

7. Media officer to liaise with senior management and with Scottish Government's media officers or with the MSP's staff to generate appropriate media interest.
    Media officer to prepare and issue news release and to co-ordinate media activity.
    Media officer to undertake social media activities to raise profile of the visit.		

8. Arrange for photographer to attend visit/launch.		
Miscellaneous		
9. Arrange name badges for all guests and staff.		
10. Arrange for suitable drinks and refreshments to be available		
11. Ensure appropriate signage is available for the event.		
12. Consider any insurance, and health and safety issues.		

Key task	Person/Team responsible	Deadline/When achieved
13. Draft any information/policy material for the event.		
14. Provide background briefing for Cabinet Secretary or Minister (and for MSP as appropriate), and offer to draft speaking notes.		
15. Draft speaking notes and background briefing paper for Chief Executive.		
16. Identify IT needs of presenters/participants, e.g. PowerPoint/screen etc., and provide IT support for event. It is strongly advised, however, that inputs should be strategic, and should be strictly controlled in length.		
Follow-up action		
17. Recognise Cabinet Secretary's or Cabinet Secretary or Minister's or the MSP's contribution to the event by sending a thank you letter. A small, obvious point, but one often overlooked by organisations, but potentially not overlooked by the Cabinet Secretary or Minister and/or by the MSP.		

Your organisation should think carefully about how best it can engage with key policy makers. Meetings with Scottish Cabinet Secretary or Ministers, with MSPs and with council leaders and lead spokespersons, and developing a programme of high profile visits/ events, can offer significant advantages for your organisation. These include helping to raise your organisation's profile, and providing opportunities to influence public policy. It can also help to safeguard and expand your organisation's business or key activities and services. These activities should play a major role in any public affairs strategy developed by your organisation.

Top Tip 3
Ensure at all times that your organisation takes a cross-party approach to its public affairs activities and campaigns.

4

Working with Individual MSPs

Working with MSPs should be at the very heart of your organisation's public affairs strategy. Which MSPs you engage with, at a specific point in time or stage in the parliamentary process, will depend upon a number of factors, including your organisation's priorities, the issues it is campaigning on, the MSPs' party allegiances and geography. Another significant factor will be an individual MSP's track record, and level of involvement, on issues relevant to your organisation and its work. One of the first things to consider in developing your public affairs strategy, and the range of activities stemming from this strategy, is how you will engage, and seek to influence, the different categories of MSPs within the Scottish Parliament. This is addressed in more detail below.

Engaging with the different types of MSPs

Two of the main categories of MSPs it is recommended your organisation should engage with are your local constituency MSP and, if your organisation delivers services, the local MSPs for each of your services. Ideally, you should try and build up your relationship with your local MSP, and encourage them to become a local champion of your work. You will find that many MSPs are supportive of, for example, local businesses and local community and voluntary sector organisations, and will be very interested to find out more about the work of such organisations within their constituencies. It has already been recommended in previous chapters that you build up your relationship with your local MSP by inviting them to visit your main office or one of your services, and by seeking regular meetings. You should also make sure that your local MSP receives copies of any newsletters or policy briefings which your organisation produces. This will provide your local MSP with a regular update about your work, and help to keep them posted on any new developments impacting upon your organisation, the sector in which it operates and upon your organisation's service users or customers.

Engaging with the Regional List MSPs will also offer your organisation important opportunities to progress aspects of its public affairs strategy. These MSPs do not have specific constituencies, but are likely to have been instructed by their party to cover certain geographical areas within the region they represent. List MSPs will, in any event, generally be interested in the activities your organisation is undertaking within the region. You should, therefore, seek to keep them fully up to date about your work. Regular contact with the list MSPs will enable your organisation to identify which specific policy areas and issues each list MSP is interested in. This will help your organisation to take a more targeted approach going forward in terms of your engagement with this particular category of MSPs.

Your organisation should also ensure that it does not overlook developing contacts with any local MSP who also serves as a Scottish Cabinet Secretary or Minister. This dual role can potentially be very beneficial to your organisation and its interests if you adopt the right approach from the outset to suit the particular circumstances. The first thing to agree internally is the capacity in which you are approaching the MSP. Is your organisation getting in touch with the MSP/Minister because they are your local MSP, or do you wish to contact them in their capacity as a Scottish Government Minister?

This is an important distinction, and getting it right is crucial because it will determine how you route your organisation's approach. If you want to contact the Minister as your local constituency MSP, you should get in touch with the Minister through the constituency office. You will find contact details on the Scottish Parliament's website. If, on the other hand, you want to get in touch with the MSP in their Ministerial capacity, you will need to contact the Ministerial office, and should allow a much longer response time. A similar distinction would apply if you are seeking to get in touch with a local MSP, who is also a front bench spokesperson for one of the Opposition parties.

Other important factors to consider in approaching an MSP/Minister is why you are approaching them in the first place, and what you want them to do on behalf of your organisation. If, for example, you just want the MSP to visit a project in their own constituency then you should approach them in their role as the local MSP, and liaise with the MSP's constituency office. One of the bonuses of having a local MSP who is a Government Minister is that, because of their high public profile from being a Minister, there is always a chance that you will get local media coverage, and also some spin-off national coverage. If, on the other hand, the Minister is leading on a new policy strategy, and one of your projects presents a strong interface with this strategy (possibly through the impact upon service users or customers), you should invite the MSP in their Ministerial role, rather than as the local MSP. As previously mentioned, if you allow sufficient time between the invite letter and the date of the proposed visit, you will significantly improve the chances of receiving a positive response to your request. With a Ministerial visit there will be opportunities to secure both national and local media coverage, and also to engage with the Minister about how the strategy will impact upon your organisation's customers or people accessing your services.

A particularly influential category of MSPs, and one which it is recommended that your organisation should cultivate good ties with, is the Convenors and Vice Convenors of the Scottish Parliament's various committees. These are usually senior and influential members of their own party, and often enjoy high standing within the Scottish Parliament itself as well. We would strongly recommend that your organisation gives high priority within its public affairs strategy to engaging with the Convenors and Vice Convenors of the committees most relevant to your work. This is vital if you are to ensure your organisation is on the policy 'radar' of these committees and, as a result, is invited to give oral, as well as written, evidence for key committee inquiries, and for the committee's Stage 1 consideration of new legislation. Securing such invites will increase the chances that your oral and written evidence will be given prominence in the inquiry and Stage 1 reports subsequently published by these committees, and debated by the Scottish Parliament. This will often help to place organisations in the best possible position to influence policy development at Scottish Government level, and legislation in the Scottish Parliament.

Developing your contacts with the committee Convenors and Vice Convenors is also a good way of getting early warning of when key business relevant to your organisation is likely to be considered in the Scottish Parliament. Securing this level of intelligence will be invaluable in helping to plan the delivery of your organisation's public affairs strategy. Advance notice will, for example, help to maximise the time available for your organisation to brief MSPs, and to make representations to Scottish Ministers, in response to new legislation and other business in the Scottish Parliament. It will also make it easier to plan and co-ordinate media activity to publicise your organisation's response to key business in the Scottish Parliament. Another advantage is that establishing good contacts with the committee Convenors and Vice Convenors will assist your organisation to gain a greater insight into how a particular committee is likely to deal with key business, and the types of policy issues and areas which will dominate its consideration of this business.

In addition, regular contacts with the Convenors and Vice Convenors could provide an insight into the dynamics within the committee, and the extent to which the members will be willing to consider the issues your organisation is seeking to raise on an objective, cross-party basis and, if necessary, to challenge their own party's position on a particular issue. This type of knowledge and intelligence will be particularly helpful if your organisation is seeking to shape and influence a piece of legislation being scrutinised by the committee. It could provide you with invaluable insights into which issues will be considered on strictly party lines, in which case you will need to consider if the issues you are raising will secure support from the Scottish Government, or if you are raising the sort of issues and amendments which will naturally generate cross-party support. Teasing out these issues will be made a lot easier if you are in regular contact with the Convenors and the Vice Convenors of the committee, as well as with individual MSPs and with the clerking team for the committee.

Some MSPs may also have a role as a Parliamentary Liaison Officer (PLO) for a specific Minister. The PLO serves as the Ministers' eyes and ears in the Parliament, watching out on behalf of the Ministers for potential issues that might arise. Knowing who the PLOs are for your key Ministers can be a useful way to bring issues to the Minster's attention.[1]

---

1. A list of the PLOs is available in a factsheet on the Scottish Parliament's website; *Scottish Parliament Fact sheet, Scottish Ministers, Law Officers and Parliamentary Liaison Officers: Session 5, (17 June 2016).*

Different types of activities

MSPs will be able to support your organisation and its work in a number of ways. Before approaching individual MSPs you should, therefore, think carefully about how best the MSP can support your organisation and the type of activities which would be most helpful in this respect. An individual MSP could, for example, lodge a motion on your behalf for a Members' Debate, or use a briefing paper your organisation has provided for a debate on a motion lodged by the Scottish Government or by one of the Opposition parties. These are all opportunities which could assist your organisation to raise key issues, and to increase your profile both as an organisation and for your work, or for your policy position on particular issues.

By engaging with your organisation at the local level, the MSP will also be more likely to highlight your work, and the best practice of any services you deliver. Opportunities to do so are often provided in debates in the Scottish Parliament, during which MSPs will often refer to local businesses, projects or services which have made an impression (both good and bad) upon them. Other important opportunities include parliamentary motions lodged by MSPs, in response to visiting an organisation and its services. Encouraging an MSP to lodge a motion about your organisation and its work will help to raise awareness about your organisation within the Scottish Parliament, and also give your organisation a chance to make the most of any media opportunities around the MSP's intervention in support of your organisation. This is an area which often works well when social media is used to raise an organisation's profile.

If you establish good relations with MSPs they might also offer to lodge a parliamentary question for written or oral answer if there are specific issues and concerns that your organisation wants to raise in the Scottish Parliament. The impact of written and oral questions will be maximised if you link it with targeted media activity, including social media. The answers generated by written and oral questions are often picked up by the media, and we would advise you to work closely with the MSP's office to make sure that you make the most of any media opportunities which may potentially arise from written or oral questions lodged on your behalf.

Your organisation will also need to work closely with individual MSPs if it wants to try and influence legislation being considered by the

Scottish Parliament. You should engage early with individual MSPs to try and persuade them to lodge amendments on your behalf at Stage 2 of the legislation. Once the amendments have been lodged by an MSP, you will be able to build upon this early engagement, and to build up a cross-party alliance of MSPs to support the amendment. Your activities in this area should include working with the sponsoring MSP to engage with the relevant Scottish Cabinet Secretary or Minister, civil servants, and with MSP members of the relevant committee at Stage 2 of the legislation, and with all MSPs before Stage 3 of the legislation.

Top Tip 4

Engaging with MSPs should be at the heart of your organisation's public affairs strategy. Give careful thought to how individual MSPs, and groups of MSPs, can support your organisation.

5

Working with Politicians
and Political Parties

As well as working with individual MSPs, your organisation must also give serious consideration to how it engages with the Scottish Government, and with the different Opposition parties. This engagement is vital if your organisation is to ensure that your public affairs strategy, and its public affairs activities and campaigns, deliver tangible outcomes such as, for example, changes in Scottish Government policy, or the launch of new policy initiatives or securing significant amendments to Scottish Government legislation. Building up cross-party alliances to support the issues you are raising, and focusing on how your organisation works with the Opposition parties, will also be important factors. These issues are considered in more detail below.

Working with the Scottish Government

Your organisation needs to give careful thought to how best it can develop its relations with the Scottish Government. It has already been suggested that your organisation should develop a programme of strategic invites to the Scottish Ministers either requesting meetings to discuss key issues, or to invite the Ministers to visit your business or services.

Your organisation should also be looking to develop its relationship with the Scottish Government's special advisers with responsibility for the policy areas most relevant to your organisation's business and its interests. Raising ideas and proposals with this group can also be very productive, because if you persuade the special advisers of the merits of your case there is a good chance that they will highlight the issues you are raising to the relevant Scottish Government Ministers. Further details about the special advisers, and their specific policy remits, can be found on the Scottish Government's website.

The importance of trying to build up a cross-party alliance of MSPs on key issues has already been highlighted, especially where your organisation is trying to influence legislation. As part of this process you also need to maximise the number of organisations which are supporting your organisation on the issues it is raising, as this will help to put pressure on individual MSPs to lend their support. However, the challenges of trying to secure your aims and objectives through a Division in the Scottish Parliament will be much more difficult if you have not informed the Scottish Government of your plans, or better still secured their support to start with. This highlights the need to cultivate your contacts with the Scottish Government, and to get the relevant Cabinet Secretaries or Ministers on board for your proposals. Securing the Cabinet Secretaries or Minister's support at an early stage, or approaching a Scottish Government backbencher to raise the issues on your behalf, are probably some of the most effective ways of trying to influence policy and legislation in the Scottish Parliament.

Apart from developing good relationships with relevant Scottish Government Ministers, your organisation should also actively develop its links with Scottish Government backbenchers. One method of doing so is to build up good contacts with the Scottish Government Whips. This group of MSPs help the Scottish Government's Business Manager to manage party business within the Scottish Parliament, and to ensure the Scottish Government wins key votes in the Scottish Parliament. If your organisation can develop these relationships, the Whips may, in certain situations, be able to give your organisation early warning about key business coming up in the Scottish Parliament, and will be able to support you, and to best advise you on how, to distribute briefing material to Scottish Government backbenchers.

Your organisation might also want to contact the Whips to sound them out about the likely response that the issues you are raising will attract from the Scottish Government benches, and from within the Scottish Parliament as a whole. Many of the political parties represented in the Scottish Parliament operate policy and research resource centres for their backbenchers within the Parliament, and we would strongly recommend that you make contact with the policy officers and researchers in these centres, and ask them to distribute any briefing material you have prepared for debates or for the consideration of legislation. They are usually only too happy to oblige.

Another aspect of developing your organisation's relationship with the Scottish Government will be liaising with the civil servants working on the policy areas in which your organisation has the greatest interest. The role of the civil servants is to support the operation of the Scottish Government, including the development and roll out of key Scottish Government policy initiatives and strategies, and the implementation of legislation. It is vital that you get your organisation on the policy radar of the civil servants. Their perception of your organisation, and your areas of interest, will be fed back by the civil servants to the Ministers, so it is important that your organisation invests time in developing good relationships with the civil servants most relevant to your organisation's work and interests.

This will also help to improve the chances that your organisation will be invited to participate in influential, high profile Scottish Government working groups established to develop and deliver different policy initiatives, strategies and legislation. Apart from being involved in these working groups, cultivating your ties with the civil servants will help to open up the channels of communication with the Scottish Government, and make it easier for your organisation to raise new initiatives and proposals, and to get a positive response from the Scottish Government where your organisation may have concerns or issues it wishes to raise.

Developing close ties with the civil servants is also likely to improve the chances that the Scottish Government will include your organisation in specific work streams around the implementation of legislation. This could include the development of the regulations and statutory guidance accompanying the primary legislation, and the development of any Subordinate legislation (also known as delegated or secondary legislation) introduced through the primary legislation.

Working with the Opposition parties

There are a number of potentially productive ways of developing your links with the Opposition parties. It is recommended that you seek meetings with the different political party leaders to update them about your organisation's work, and to discuss key issues. You might want to combine a meeting request with a visit to your business, or to one of your projects or services, as this will give the relevant political party leader an opportunity to secure some media interest and local publicity. This will often be an important factor in persuading the political parties' leaders to respond positively to your organisation's request.

Your organisation should also arrange a series of meetings/visits for the party spokespersons for the policy areas most relevant to your organisation's work and interests. These contacts will be crucial and it is, therefore, important that your organisation invests some time in building up your relationships with the respective political party spokespersons. You want the spokespersons, in particular, to be aware of your organisation's work, your aims and objectives and the policy areas in which you are most active. Establishing this level of relationship will help to ensure that, whenever the Scottish Parliament is focusing on policy areas and issues relevant to your organisation and its work, the respective party spokespersons will be more likely to engage with your organisation on these matters at an early stage.

Your organisation should also give further thought to ways in which it can influence the respective political parties' internal group meetings. These are usually held weekly in the Scottish Parliament, and you should contact the relevant spokespersons, or the party's Chief Whip or business manager, to offer to provide an input at this meeting. This request should be made on a cross-party basis to avoid accusations of bias, and the invite should, therefore, be extended to all of the political parties represented in the Scottish Parliament.

As indicated above, many of the Opposition parties also have their own policy and research centres in the Scottish Parliament, which offer support and resources to their MSPs. The duties and responsibilities of these policy and research centres usually include preparing briefing material for debates in the Scottish Parliament, or for the consideration of legislation. The researchers and policy officers staffing these centres will usually be keen to receive briefings for debates and legislation from external bodies and agencies, including businesses, public bodies, umbrella organisations and community and voluntary organisations. If you contact the staff they will often offer to circulate any briefing for you to their party's MSPs, or advise you on how best to take a targeted approach to ensuring that your briefing goes to those MSPs most interested in the issues your organisation wishes to raise.

Influencing the political parties' manifestos

Elections to the Scottish Parliament offer significant opportunities for organisations to influence the policy positions of the different political parties by engaging with these parties as they develop their manifestos for the forthcoming elections. Each party has its own approach to the formulation and drafting of manifestos. While some actively seek the input of external organisations and agencies and will conduct an extensive consultation exercise with the latter, involving meetings, surveys and focus groups, other parties will focus their engagement much more narrowly.

The parties begin the process of developing their manifestos at different times, and if your organisation wishes to contribute ideas to the parties' manifestos, it is strongly advised that you make early contact with the different parties to seek clarification of the timescales involved, and the processes which they will follow in formulating their manifestos. It is also advised that you take a cross-party approach and that, if you seek to provide input to the manifesto of one party, you should also, as best practice, provide input to the manifestos of the other parties. This will defend your organisation from any accusations of political bias which could limit the impact of your organisation's influencing strategy. This would be a particular concern if the party with which your organisation becomes closely associated fails to win the election. Adopting a cross-party approach will also help your organisation to maximise its impact in the key policy debates around the Scottish Parliament election campaign.

Working with the parties' media officers

One area which you must not neglect in working with all of the political parties in the Scottish Parliament is making the most of any media opportunities to highlight your organisation's work, as well as any key issues on which your organisation is campaigning. Raising your organisation's profile in these areas is vital, and will help to maximise the opportunities for your organisation's public affairs strategy, and related public affairs activities, to deliver tangible outcomes. This, however, will often depend ultimately upon the extent to which your organisation can demonstrate persuasively that there is substance, including proven best practice and evidence, underpinning the issues you are raising.

It is also essential that your organisation takes a cross-party approach to media opportunities as appropriate. If, for example, a Scottish Government Minister has agreed to give the keynote speech at an event to open new premises for one of your organisation's businesses, projects or services, and the local constituency MSP is also due to provide an input, you should seek to refer to both in any news release. In this context, we would recommend that you draft a news release outlining the background to the event, and including quotes from your chief officer, from the Scottish Government Minister and from the local MSP (especially if they are from one of the Opposition parties). You should then work with the Minister's media team and the local MSP's office to get them to sign off the quotes (which they will often wish to fine tune), and to then finalise the news release with any changes they have requested. You should also work with these contacts to make the most of opportunities presented by social media.

Taking this cross-party approach will help your organisation to avoid any accusations of political bias, and is essential if you want to establish solid relationships of trust with all of the political parties in the Scottish Parliament. It will also help to minimise the risks that your organisation gets caught up inadvertently in any political crossfire between different parties. In this respect, you should bear in mind that inviting the Minister to visit another MSP's constituency – which they are completely entitled to do – can create tensions with the local constituency MSP (particularly if they represent different political parties) if not properly managed from the outset. Factoring this into your planning for an event will help to minimise, if not eradicate, such tensions.

To take another example, if an opposition MSP has agreed to lodge amendments on your organisation's behalf to a parliamentary Bill, you should consider issuing a news release to raise the profile of the issues you are seeking to raise. To try and persuade the Minister to accept the amendments we would recommend that you send the Minister a copy of the amendments and the supporting briefing as early as possible in the legislative process. As best practice you should also send the Minister a copy of the news release which you will be issuing in support of the amendments. Taking action in these areas will help to ensure that the Minister and their officials do not get caught on the back foot by the issues you are raising. This, in turn, might make the Minister more receptive to the amendments, and more likely to announce concessions in response to your organisation's amendments.

Publicity – good and bad – is often the mother of political change in parliaments across the world, and the Scottish Parliament is often no different in this respect. Politicians are extremely sensitive to publicity, and many will not forget those who have contributed to their embarrassment. Avoid this scenario as much as you can. That said, sometimes it is inevitable that your organisation will, by necessity, have to raise issues which will not be welcomed by the Scottish Government, and which could bring you into disagreement with the Scottish Ministers. The secret is to take a 'no surprises' approach, and raise these issues in a way which does not close down the essential channels of communication with the Scottish Government that are going to be critical to any successful resolution of the issues your organisation is raising. How your organisation manages its media work and publicity around such issues will be an important part of this process.

In this context, while the use of publicity is essential to the work of many organisations across the different sectors, it is important to recognise that this requires careful and responsible management. Most businesses, public bodies and community and voluntary organisations, for example, will not wish, and will not be able under their memorandum and articles of association or mission statements, to be partisan, and to support one or other of the political parties. It is, therefore, essential that your organisation takes a balanced, cross-party approach to your media work.

Admittedly, there will be times when your organisation and its partners have legitimate reasons for publicly criticising some aspect of Scottish Government policy regardless of which party is in power. In this context, giving the Scottish Government a copy of your news release in advance will often help to secure a more thoughtful, positive response from the Scottish Government. It will also serve to underline the fact that your organisation is committed to working constructively and on a cross-party basis, and is seeking to raise issues that are of public concern and which should be considered on their merit. This approach, based on respect and mutuality, has been found to open up, and/or maintain, useful channels of communication between organisations and the Scottish Government on particular issues.

Top Tip 5

Engaging with the Scottish Government, and with the opposition parties, will be vital to your organisation's public affairs strategy. Apart from the Scottish Ministers, engage with the Scottish Ministers' Parliamentary Liaison Officers and special advisers, and with the leaders and key spokespersons of the Opposition parties, to ensure your organisation's strategy delivers tangible outcomes.

Responding to Consultations

Which bodies consult?

The Scottish Government regularly launches consultations on issues covering a wide range of public policy areas. Apart from providing your organisation with opportunities to raise key issues and concerns and to influence public policy, Scottish Government consultations will also offer opportunities to raise your organisation's profile with Scottish Government Ministers, with Scottish Government officials, with the Opposition parties and with individual MSPs. Consultations may also be launched by committees, and are usually required for Members' Bills.

Details of Government consultations can be found on the 'consultation' section of the Scottish Government's website. You should get into the habit of regularly looking at the consultation section on the Scottish Government's website for details of any consultations likely to impact upon your organisation and its work. This section is highly accessible, and you should be able to identify any relevant consultations in a matter of minutes. It really is as simple as that.

Alternatively, if you cannot spare even a short time to look at the consultation section on the Scottish Government's website for a few minutes each day, your organisation can sign up to receive regular e-mail updates from the Scottish Government about new consultations, and other key policy initiative and developments. The key thing is that the alert is received by someone in your organisation who will be able to update colleagues about the consultation, and to take responsibility for submitting a response on behalf of the organisation.

Depending upon the sector your organisation works within, you can also find out useful information about ongoing consultations from the websites/e-mail updates of any relevant membership organisations to which your organisation belongs. For the community and voluntary sector this might include, for example, the websites of the Scottish Council for Voluntary Organisations, YouthLink Scotland and Scottish Environment Link. In many cases these umbrella organisations will submit responses to specific Scottish Government consultations on behalf of their members. They will also encourage and support member organisations to submit their own responses, and to highlight common themes in their responses.

You should also look out for UK Government consultations on issues which will impact on Scotland, and/or are relevant to your organisation's work and interests. Notification of these consultations can be found on various UK Government websites, and in particular on the various departmental websites of the UK Government. You will know which UK Government Ministries are most involved in the areas of your organisation's work, and these should be prioritised.

Regulatory bodies and other agencies such as, for example, the Office of the Scottish Charity Regulator, the Scottish Environment Protection Agency and the Scottish Law Commission also sometimes launch consultations on different issues, and it is recommended that your organisation keeps an eye out for any consultations regulatory bodies and other agencies may have launched which cover aspects of your work. This is an area in which membership organisations should be actively seeking to keep their members up to date, and to encourage them to contribute to the membership organisation's response and/or to submit responses on behalf of their own, individual organisations.

The Scottish Government's consultation process

The aim of these consultations is generally to seek the views of key stakeholders in the relevant sectors, on specific policy proposals, changes and strategies, as well as on draft legislation and regulations. The Scottish Government consultation documents generally contain a list of questions, which stakeholders are requested to complete and return to the relevant policy department within the Scottish Government. Most of the consultations can be responded to on-line. You should answer as many of the questions as possible because all responses are analysed, and some of the questions often require a simple 'yes or no' answer. You must also complete the Respondent Information Form with details of your organisation, including details of the relevant contact person.

The Scottish Government officials running the consultations want to try and maximise the number of responses they receive, and are usually very helpful. The consultation documents contain contact details for the lead officials, and you should not hesitate to get in touch with these officials if you require further information about any of the issues raised in the consultation document. Ideally, you should submit your consultation response well before the close of the consultation deadline. If this does not prove possible, you should contact the relevant official as early as possible to explain that your organisation wants to submit a response, but will struggle to meet the deadline and to try and negotiate an extension. In many cases the officials will be willing to provide a short extension if it helps to increase the number of responses received to the consultation. That said, your organisation's best practice should be to commit to respond to all consultations within the prescribed deadline, and to ensure that your organisation has appropriate 'sign-off' procedures in place internally to achieve this aim.

With high profile consultations, the Scottish Government will often run consultation events to help inform the consultation process, and to maximise the number of responses received. These events offer useful opportunities to find out more about the consultation proposals, and about how these proposals will impact upon key stakeholders. It is strongly advised that your organisation tries to send a representative to attend such events, because even if your organisation is already up to speed on the details of the consultation, these events often serve as a useful information exchange with the Scottish Government and with peer organisations. This will enable your organisation to assess how other organisations view the Scottish Government's proposals, and also to identify possible gaps where your organisation could lead its sector on key issues. Your organisation might also want to use the occasion of a consultation event to 'road test' some of the issues it will be seeking to raise in its consultation response. By doing so, this could help your organisation to identify the strengths, as well as any potential weaknesses, in the issues it is seeking to raise with the Scottish Government. This, in turn, could support your organisation to strengthen the ways in which it will present key issues within its overall consultation response. Using such opportunities to improve your organisation's consultation response will increase the chances that it will receive a positive response from the Scottish Government, and influence policy development.

Where your parliamentary monitoring, and/or engagement with Scottish Government Ministers, has identified that the Scottish Government will be launching a new consultation, you should consider making an early approach to the relevant Scottish Government Minister to suggest launching the consultation at your business/projects/ services, or to host one of the consultation events at your business/ project/service. This will help to boost your profile on the areas of your work covered by the consultation, and also give your organisation an opportunity to support the consultation process, which will be appreciated by the Minister and their officials. It could also help to ensure that your organisation influences and informs the consultation process.

Making your consultation response stand out

Scottish Government consultations often attract hundreds of responses from organisations, agencies and from individuals. Ensuring that your organisation's response stands out for the right reasons is, therefore, going to be a challenge.

It is recommended that, in addition to your answers to the questions outlined in the consultation document, for ease of reference you might also want to include a summary of the issues you wish to raise at the beginning of your response. It may also be worth highlighting your key issues to the relevant Scottish Government Minister or Ministers, if you think your comments may prove particularly controversial, or, in the case of legislation, may require significant amendments from the Scottish Government. Alternatively, passing your consultation response to the Special Adviser or the Parliamentary Liaison Officer may help ensure your concerns feature on the policy radar of Scottish Government Ministers in relation to the policy issues covered by the consultation.

A good consultation response will draw upon the best practice of your organisation, and also draw upon any evidence and evaluations which are available to support your arguments. A thoughtful response will also pose its own questions, and raise issues which are not necessarily addressed, or developed in any depth, within the Scottish Government's consultation document, but that are definitely relevant. This will alert the Scottish Government to any issues they have missed, or not given sufficient weight to, in the consultation document. It could be, for example, that the consultation does not clearly draw out the interface between the Scottish Government's policy proposals outlined in the consultation and other existing Scottish Government policy streams.

Follow-up action

The Scottish Government will analyse the responses received to the consultation, and will often publish reports summarising the main issues highlighted in the responses received, and confirming how they propose to take forward the proposals outlined in the consultation documents. Unfortunately, such reports, including the quotes provided by stakeholders, are often anonymised so with some reports you will have to cross refer back to your consultation response to identify which issues you raised are reflected in the report.

If the consultation leads to the introduction of new legislation, you should revisit your response to the original consultation, and then look at the draft legislation to see how many of the issues you raised were taken on board. This process should help to shape and inform your organisation's response to the legislation in the Scottish Parliament.

An important point to bear in mind here is that, although your organisation previously submitted a consultation response to the Scottish Government and to its officials, you must not assume that MSPs on the Scottish Parliament committee dealing with the legislation will be aware of any issues/concerns you raised previously in your consultation response. In this context, it is important to bear in mind that in many ways you are starting from scratch, and from experience this is often no bad thing. So feel free to raise with MSPs on the relevant committee any issues which your organisation does not believe have been properly addressed through the original Scottish Government consultation.

The MSPs will consider the issues you raise on their merit, and they might support them, which will give your organisation a further opportunity to influence and shape the Scottish Government's legislative proposals.

Scottish Parliament consultations usually take the form of parliamentary inquiries. These can be on a range of policy issues and areas, and can include Stage 1 inquiries into the general principles of legislation. Responding to Scottish Parliamentary consultations and inquiries should be, or should become, a major part of your organisation's public affairs strategy.

In this respect, it is worth considering that Scottish Government consultations are, by their nature, controlled by the Scottish Government, which ultimately decides which, if any, issues raised in stakeholders' responses it wants to accept, and to reflect in the proposals it takes forward. Sometimes very few issues raised by stakeholders are accepted. In this scenario you are then forced to rely on the parliamentary process, after the Scottish Government has introduced legislation based on its original consultation, to try and influence the Scottish Government's proposals.

Against this background, consultations launched by the Scottish Parliament for specific inquiries or at Stage 1 of legislation, often offer organisations greater scope for influencing the Scottish Government's policy and legislative proposals, than the original Scottish Government consultation. This is because the Scottish Government's legislation and/or policy strategies will be subject to scrutiny by committees within the Scottish Parliament.

The parliamentary scrutiny of legislation will offer organisations opportunities to shape the Scottish Government's proposals. The committees' scrutiny will enable your organisation to do so if the issues you are raising are well thought out and persuasively argued, and backed up by robust evidence and best practice. It will also help if your organisation is working in partnership, and is expressing issues and concerns raised contemporaneously by other organisations and agencies which have also submitted evidence to the committee.

Top Tip 6
Responding to consultations will provide important opportunities for your organisation to contribute to key policy debates, and to raise your organisation's profile with policy makers.

7

Influencing Scottish Parliamentary Committees

A lot of key business in the Scottish Parliament is channeled through the parliamentary committees. These committees consist of small groups of Members who have been appointed by their parties and by the Scottish Parliament to meet regularly (either weekly or fortnightly and usually on a Tuesday, Wednesday or Thursday morning). The purpose of the committees, according to the guide to their work available on the Scottish Parliament's website, is to "scrutinise the work of the Scottish Government, conduct inquiries into subjects within their remit and examine legislation, including bills and subordinate legislation[1]".

It is, therefore, essential that your organisation's public affairs strategy, if the aim of this strategy is to shape and influence public policy and legislation in the Scottish Parliament, includes a strong focus on engaging with these committees.

Some committees are required by the Standing Orders of the Scottish Parliament. These are the following committees:

- Delegated Powers and Law Reform Committee
- Equal Opportunities Committee
- European and External Relations Committee
- Finance Committee
- Public Audit Committee
- Public Petitions Committee
- Standards, Procedures and Public Appointments Committee

---

1. Scottish Parliament, Fact sheet 'Scottish Parliament committees – what are they and what do they do?', Scottish Parliament website.

The Scottish Parliament also agrees on a number of other committees to deal with a particular subject or area, which may match Ministerial portfolios, but are not required to do so. These are known as subject committees.

The committees pages on the Scottish Parliament's website will provide details of the current committees and their remits.

The subject committees in the Scottish Parliament are currently as follows:

- Economy, Jobs and Fair Work Committee
- Education and Skills Committee
- Environment, Climate Change and Land Reform Committee
- Health and Sport Committee
- Justice Committee
- Local Government and Communities Committee
- Rural Economy and Connectivity Committee
- Social Security Committee

Sometimes the Scottish Parliament establishes committees on a short life basis to undertake scrutiny of specific legislation, such as, for example, the Scotland Bill Committee which considered the UK Government's Scotland Bill in 2011-12.

Your organisation must decide which of the Scottish Parliamentary committees to engage with, and to seek to influence. This will depend upon the type of organisation you work for, the sector in which your organisation operates, the policy and strategic areas in which your organisation works, and your organisation's aims and objectives, as well as the remit of each committee and the parliamentary business for which each individual committee is responsible.

The main areas of the individual committee's work which your organisation could potentially get the most involved in are the committees' scrutiny of legislation, and the committees' launch of parliamentary inquiries into a wide range of subjects and issues falling within the remit of individual committees. These areas can present major work streams for organisations, and ones which, if progressed effectively, can provide your organisation with important opportunities to raise its profile, and to shape and influence significant parliamentary business impacting upon its work and interests.

Committees' home pages

Committees' work programmes, including the previous committees' legacy papers, can be accessed on the home pages for each committee on the Scottish Parliament's website. The committee home pages are full of information, including the remit and responsibilities of the committee, and details of its membership and of the clerking team.

The committee home pages will confirm current business, and also give you a good steer about what key business is coming up, including the timetable for the different stages of parliamentary legislation being considered by the committee, as well as details of committee inquiries. You can also access copies of the Official Report from previous committee sittings, the agendas and relevant documents for specific committee sittings, as well as copies of reports published by the committee.

Scanning and analysing the home pages of Scottish Parliamentary committees relevant to your organisation and to its work and interests should become an integral part of your parliamentary monitoring processes. If, however, your organisation has only limited capacity for parliamentary monitoring, you can register for committee updates through the committee home pages. These will keep you posted on key business coming up in the different committees most relevant to your organisation and its work. You can also book seats to attend committee meetings through the committees' home pages on the Scottish Parliament's website.

The Committee's Work Programme

At the end of each Scottish Parliament, when the parliament is dissolved and the politicians go off to fight the election, you should use the time around the parliamentary 'pre-election period' to familiarise yourself with the legacy papers drafted by the outgoing committees. These legacy papers are designed to help inform the work of the new committees which will be established after the Scottish Parliamentary Elections, and the new crop of MSPs have been sworn in and the Scottish Parliament has voted to establish the new committees.

Keep a careful eye out for any changes to the titles and remits of existing committees, and also to the dissolution of certain committees and to the setting up of new committees. It is worth bearing in mind that such changes could be accompanied by the appointment of new parliamentary staff, particularly to the clerking teams, supporting the work of the committees. Where such personnel changes occur it is important that your organisation engages with the committee's new staff members to ensure that they are aware of your organisation and its work, and of the committee business in which your organisation has an interest.

Taking the time to familiarise yourselves with the legacy papers of the committees focusing on areas central to your organisation's work, and to your aims and objectives, will provide your organisation with real scope to position itself strategically at an early stage with the new committees and with their MSP members and clerking teams. It will also enable your organisation to help shape and inform the committees' work programmes going forward.

This is a prime opportunity to ensure that your organisation's key issues and concerns are taken up by the committee as integral parts of its work programme. Achieving this objective could offer major advantages for your organisation, including the chance to influence the committees' policy agendas by persuading them to focus on the main issues your organisation has prioritised.

The key to achieving this objective is to contact the Convenor and the members of the committee, as well as the clerks, and to highlight the issues and concerns your organisation wants to raise, and their synergy with the relevant aspects of the legacy paper and with the key business likely to dominate the new parliament and the work of its committees.

You should contact the committee as soon as its structure and membership are announced (membership is proposed through a motion lodged by the Parliamentary Bureau, and must then be approved by a meeting of the whole Scottish Parliament), and request an early meeting with the committee to discuss these areas. Ideally, your organisation should try and secure an invite to provide an input at one of the committee away days, which committees tend to hold shortly after being established to discuss and agree their work programmes going forward. When you contact the committee your organisation should also highlight its availability and willingness to provide evidence, or to host project visits, to help inform the committee's consideration of key issues falling within its remit.

If your organisation has particular expertise in a policy area, and the committee will be giving this policy area priority, there might also be opportunities to approach the committee about registering as a Committee Adviser or Research Consultant to help support the work of the committee on a particular topic or area. Further details about how to become a Committee Adviser or Research Consultant can be found on the committee's home pages.

Even if your organisation's approach is politely declined, contacting the committee early at the beginning of a new parliament may help to get your organisation on the committee's policy radar, and help to maximise the chances of your organisation being given opportunities to give oral evidence in future.

When progressing this approach it is strongly advised that you make sure the clerks are copied in to any correspondence, as the new Convenor, Deputy Convenor and other members of the committee will rely on the clerks' input in helping to develop the committee's new work programme. Part of that process will be looking at the legacy paper of the previous committee, and assessing and agreeing what aspects, if any, of the legacy paper should be adapted in the new work programme.

Trying to support the work of the committees by drawing their attention to key issues and areas of work should be an important area of your organisation's public affairs strategy, and one which should be given some priority. Significant opportunities like these to proactively influence the work of committees do not come around very often in the parliamentary calendar. These opportunities should be eagerly anticipated and seized upon because once the committee has agreed its work programme for the parliamentary session, then the committee's scope for looking at other issues outside its work programme – regardless of how pressing or meritorious – will be much more limited.

Another key landmark in trying to influence the work programmes of parliamentary committees is at the start of each new parliamentary session, with the First Minister's statement to the Scottish Parliament on the Scottish Government's Programme for Government. This usually occurs in September, and if your organisation wants to try and take advantage of any room for manoeuvre within the committee's existing work programme for new initiatives, this is the time to try and do so. It is recommended that you make contact with the Convenor and the clerks before the start of the new session, and to set out which issues you wish to raise, and how you would suggest the committee can best deal with these issues. It could, for example, be a proposal for a short-term inquiry on an issue which has become high profile and urgent since the committee first drafted its initial work programme, or an invite for the committee to visit one of your projects to find out more about how a particular policy strategy or piece of legislation being considered by the committee will impact upon your organisation, its work and upon your customers or those accessing your services.

Cultivating ties with Committees

Once your organisation has identified which committees will take lead responsibility for considering key areas of work in which you have an interest, your organisation needs to take stock of how strong your relationships are with the Convenors, the membership and clerking teams for these particular committees.

Does the membership of the committee include, for example, MSPs whom your organisation already has good relations, or are you really starting out from scratch?

It is important to build upon any existing relationships, and to seek early meetings with these MSPs to find out more about the key issues for the committee on specific areas of its work, and about the likely dynamic within the committees your organisation is seeking to engage with. How cross-party will the MSPs be in their approach, for example, within the committee or will they approach all issues on party lines?

Where you do not have existing contacts with members of the committee, you should look at the background and interests of individual members and identify any links or connections with your organisation and the issues you are seeking to raise, and with your particular sector generally. You should also consider if the membership includes your local MSP, or a member for the Regional List covering the area in which your organisation is based or operates. You should contact these MSPs and seek early meetings either in the Scottish Parliament, or at one of your projects or businesses, to update them about your organisation's work and to highlight the issues you will be raising in response to the committee's work programme.

If there is no majority for a particular party within the committee then you need to consider how best to build up a cross-party alliance behind any issues you are raising. This will be particularly important where you are seeking to persuade a committee to accept amendments to a parliamentary Bill. The same considerations will apply where a party has a majority within the committee. Against this background, you will need to try even harder to persuade a member of the majority party to either lodge amendments on your behalf, or to support amendments lodged by opposition MSPs.

Committee's scrutiny of legislation

Another major area where your organisation should seek to engage with the committees is in their scrutiny of parliamentary legislation relevant to your organisation and its work.

If the Scottish Government, or a committee, introduces legislation which is relevant to your organisation and its interests, or if an MSP introduces a Members' Bill in a key policy area for your organisation's work and the Bill has been given time in the parliamentary timetable, you should strongly consider giving priority to responding to this legislation. Focusing on the relevant committees will be critical to the success of your organisation's attempts to influence key legislation impacting upon its work and interests.

Responding to parliamentary legislation is considered in detail in Chapters 8 and 9 below. By way of a quick overview of the key stages of the committees' work on legislation and in which your organisation should seek to get involved, Stage 1 of the legislative process in the Scottish Parliament focuses on evidence gathering and on scrutiny of the general principles of the legislation, while Stage 2 and Stage 3 of the legislation focus on substantive amendments to the legislation.

Ensuring that your organisation is involved in all stages of significant legislation impacting upon its work should be at the very heart of your organisation's public affairs strategy. It will help to raise your organisation's profile on key issues, and present opportunities to try and improve the legislation to reflect issues and concerns raised by your organisation.

Other parliamentary inquiries

Another important dimension of the work of the parliamentary committees is their scrutiny of the Scottish Government's policies and strategies, and of other issues falling within their remit. These areas are usually addressed through parliamentary inquiries, which can consist of short life evidence sessions, or more in-depth investigations into particular issues or aspects of government policy.

By analysing the committee's work programme, and by keeping a close eye on the committee's homepage or on its e-mail updates, your organisation should be able to identify the inquiries likely to be relevant to its work, and to plan accordingly.

One of the key activities in this area is to draft your organisation's written evidence for any inquiries. The committee normally calls for a maximum of four pages of evidence, and sets questions to be addressed in stakeholders' written evidence. Any organisation or agency or individual, with an interest in the legislation, can submit written evidence.

Your organisation should seek to submit its written evidence as early as possible, as this will have a bearing on whether or not your organisation gets invited to give oral evidence. The sooner you get your written evidence lodged, the longer it will appear on the Scottish Parliament's website (on the committee's home page), which will be useful in terms of raising your organisation's profile.

Apart from submitting your evidence to the clerks to the committee, you should also write to the Convenor and Vice-Convenor of the committee, along with the other members of the committee, attaching a copy of your organisation's evidence, and highlighting your main issues and concerns in a covering letter. You should also consider following this up with requests to meet individual members of the committee to discuss the key issues your organisation is raising. This will help to maximise the chances of these issues featuring in the committee's final report.

You need to ensure that your evidence stands out for the right reasons, so try and ensure that your written evidence is persuasive and well presented, and is backed up by robust best practice and evidence. The aim here is to ensure that your evidence features prominently in the committee's final report. You should also consider making a bid, on the back of your organisation's written evidence, to persuade the committee to send a Reporting Group to your business or to one of your projects/services to help inform their consideration of the issues featured in the legislation or in the inquiry. The more persuasive and thoughtful you can make your evidence, the more chance there is that your organisation will be invited to give oral evidence to the committee.

Giving oral evidence

Being asked to give oral evidence to a Scottish Parliamentary inquiry can be a daunting experience, but if your organisation prepares properly the evidence session can offer your organisation significant opportunities to dominate the policy debates around the inquiry, and for your evidence to feature heavily in the committee's final report.

After looking at the remit for the inquiry, and at the specific areas which your evidence session will focus on, your organisation needs to take a view on who would be best placed to give evidence on its behalf in the evidence session. If the session will focus on policy issues then it would be best for a senior manager with a good understanding of the policy context to give the evidence. Alternatively, if the session will focus on service/business issues then you would be advised to get your chief officer or another senior manager from the operational side of your organisation to give evidence.

Some committees will outline the questions they want answered in their invite to give evidence, which is helpful. Unfortunately, in many cases knowing which path a committee will follow with its lines of questioning can be difficult to predict even at the best of times, and even where the questions are confirmed in advance. It is, therefore, advised that you start your organisation's preparation by sounding out the clerks to get a sense from them of what the key themes and questions are likely to be during the evidence session. In most cases the clerks will only be able to give some general pointers, as a lot will depend upon how hands-on the Convenor is likely to be in steering the committee through the main themes. Other important factors will be the particular policy interests, and the level of engagement, of the individual MSPs on the committee.

To try and minimise the risks of any policy 'curve balls', it is important that you know your audiences. It is, therefore, strongly advised that, apart from contacting the clerks before the evidence session, you also speak to your MSP contacts on the committee to try and find out which members of the committee have particular issues and policy areas that they are likely to raise. As part of your organisation's preparation for the oral evidence session, it is recommended that you compile an evidence pack of the written evidence previously submitted by other organisations and individuals, prioritising the written evidence raising significant issues for your organisation. In addition, it is worth looking at what previous witnesses said in their oral evidence, as this may provide strong indicators of the types of issues of most interest to the committee, and give your organisation an opportunity to prepare a response in anticipation of these issues being revisited by the committee.

The person giving evidence on behalf of your organisation should also acquaint/reacquaint themselves with the written evidence submitted previously by your organisation, as a committee member may without any warning put your representative on the spot by asking a specific question/supplementary question about your evidence. It is, therefore, advisable, that your organisation's representative fully understands the key issues they are to prioritise and to raise, and the evidence they are going rely on. In this respect, your organisation might want to agree internally the three key points which it wants its representative to get across to the committee during the evidence session.

It is also strongly recommended that your organisation ensures that time has been set aside in which the spokesperson can run through their potential 'answers' and the issues they wish to raise. Ideally, your organisation should arrange for its communications and/or policy staff to run a 'mock' evidence session with the spokesperson to try and anticipate the type of questions and issues on which the committee will concentrate. Such sessions can be helpful in supporting your organisation's representative to fine tune their answers.

Debates on committee reports

After the committee has taken written and oral evidence for its inquiry, it will then publish a final report. The report will include an analysis and review of all of the evidence received by the committee, and feature a number of conclusions and recommendations. If your organisation's evidence has been persuasive and perceptive, and if you have followed up by engaging with individual members of the committee and with the clerking team, then this will help to ensure that the key issues raised by your organisation are given prominence in the committee's final report.

Once the committee has published its report, the Scottish Government will usually publish its response to the committee's report and recommendations. The Scottish Parliament will then debate the committee's report. This debate will afford your organisation a further opportunity to engage with MSPs of all parties on the key issues you have raised during the inquiry.

To maximise the impact of your evidence you should circulate it to MSPs before the debate. Your options are to send your evidence, or a short, concise briefing paper based upon your evidence and updated to reflect the committee's key findings and the Scottish Government's response, to all MSPs or to take a more targeted approach. Both approaches offer advantages and disadvantages.

Sending a briefing out to all MSPs will potentially raise your organisation's profile, and highlight the issues and concerns upon which you wish to influence the Scottish Government and MSPs. The downside is that MSPs might be reluctant to rely on a briefing paper or evidence which has been widely circulated, as understandably they want their contribution to the debate to have a certain originality and uniqueness. They might also want to 'champion' particular issues on behalf of organisations to which they have pre-existing links.

If you are not prepared to take the risks associated with a general mailing to MSPs, then your organisation should take a more targeted approach to briefing MSPs. In this respect, it is advised that your organisation sends a copy of its briefing to the relevant Minister/ Ministers, and then briefs MSP contacts on different issues around the inquiry. It would be best to focus on MSPs who are members of the committee, or to focus on local MSPs or on MSPs with an existing connection to your organisation.

Top Tip 7
Cultivate your contacts with the Convenors and the MSPs on the committees most relevant to your organisation's work, and with the clerking teams to those committees. This will help your organisation to shape and influence key policy inquiries and legislation being dealt with by the committees.

8

Engaging with the Legislative Process: Pre-Legislation to Stage 1

Legislation impacts upon us all, and in many different ways. Legislation or Statute law, along with the common law, affects various aspects of our lives. And what greater, more tangible outcome could there be for an organisation's public affairs strategy than to have raised public awareness on a particular issue or issues, to have raised the organisation's profile and to have changed the law for the better. Public affairs strategies literally do not come much better than that, or present better outcomes.

If your organisation wants to significantly raise the level of its public affairs work, it should consider how it can help to shape and influence legislation being considered by the Scottish Parliament.

Different sectors have tended to enjoy varying degrees of success in their attempts to shape and influence Scottish Government legislation. The Convention of Scottish Local Authorities (COSLA), which represents most of Scotland's local authorities, has enjoyed significant success in this area. Recently, this has owed a lot to the Scottish Government and COSLA being partners under the Concordat arrangements. Another organisation which has consistently had a major impact in influencing Scottish Government policy initiatives, and in amending Scottish Government legislation in the Scottish Parliament, is the Law Society of Scotland.

By contrast, other organisations and sectors have been less successful in their attempts to shape Scottish Government legislation. Over the years, community and voluntary organisations have often been very frustrated by their lack of success in changing legislation, despite an apparently positive reception from politicians for their aims and objectives, and for their work and for many of their campaigns.

And yet it does not have to be like that. The community and voluntary sector has significant strength and vitality, and could offer proven expertise and in-depth experience to help inform and improve most parliamentary legislation. The problems are, however, that community and voluntary organisations do not find out about the legislation. In particular community and voluntary organisations can be very active in pre-legislative consultations and at Stage 1 of the Bill, raising a whole series of important issues. However, because they do not progress their scrutiny of the Bill to Stage 2 these concerns do not lead to legislative change unless they are picked up and adopted by the Government or by Opposition MSPs at Stage 2 of the legislation.

Which legislation should your organisation respond to?

The answer quite simply is any legislation likely to impact upon your organisation, and its work either in terms of the businesses it runs, the services its delivers and any groups its supports, or the policy issues upon which it campaigns or in which it has an interest.

Ideally, your organisation should, using the criteria above, be seeking to respond to any of the following types of legislation:

- Scottish Government ('Government') Bills introduced to progress and implement Scottish Government policy and strategic priorities;
- Subordinate legislation, mainly in the form of regulations and orders, introduced by statutory instruments through powers contained in primary legislation. These regulations and orders make an important contribution to the implementation and revision of primary legislation;
- Committee Bills introduced by individual Scottish Parliamentary committees to progress and implement policy and strategic priorities identified by the committee itself, or by the Scottish Parliament as a whole (a Committee Bill can also be introduced in response to a request from an MSP); and

- Members' Bills introduced by an MSP on a particular issue or issues, and given parliamentary time in which to be progressed.

This chapter, and the next chapter, look at how your organisation's public affairs strategy and activities can help to shape and influence Government and Committee Bills. Members' Bills are dealt with separately in Chapter 10. Private Bills are beyond the scope of this guide. Further information about Private Bills can be found in the Scottish Parliament's Guidance on Public Bills, which defines a Private Bill as being "introduced by private individual or bodies seeking powers or benefits in excess of or in conflict with the general law"[1].

The key stages of a Government Bill are the consultation stage held by the Scottish Government, and Stages 1, 2 and 3 all of which are undertaken in the Scottish Parliament. The overall process is the same for Committee Bills, except that there would not normally be a pre-legislative, consultation stage undertaken by the Scottish Government. The Bills will then receive Royal Assent and become Acts, and enter the Statute Book. This chapter, and the following chapter, provide an overview of the legislative process in the Scottish Parliament, and suggest ways in which your organisation could respond effectively to each stage in the legislative process.

In outline, procedure for a Scottish Parliament bill usually consists of four stages:

Pre-legislative consultation – either launched by the Scottish Government, by a Scottish Parliamentary Committee or by an individual MSP, depending upon where the proposals for the legislation originate.

Stage 1 – A committee scrutinises the general principles of the Bill, a process which includes taking written and oral evidence from the Scottish Government, and from various organisations and individuals. The committee produces its Stage 1 report on the general principles of the Bill, which is then debated by the Scottish Parliament before deciding if it supports the legislation.

---

1. Scottish Parliament, Guidance on Public Bills, Session 5 Edition (Version 1, June 2016).

Stage 2 – A parliamentary committee undertakes line by line scrutiny of the Bill, and considers, and if necessary debates, amendments to the Bill, which are accepted or rejected.

Stage 3 – The whole Scottish Parliament considers further amendments to the Bill which are accepted or rejected and, after a short debate, the Scottish Parliament decides whether to pass or reject the Bill.

If a Bill is passed at Stage 3, it will be submitted for Royal Assent, unless a successful challenge is mounted within a four week period of the Bill being passed based on the grounds that it is outside the legislative competence of the Scottish Parliament. After the Bill has received Royal Assent it becomes an Act of the Scottish Parliament.

Further information about the legislative process in the Scottish Parliament can be found in the Scottish Parliament's Guidance on Public Bills, and in its Standing Orders, which are available on the Scottish Parliament's website.

The public affairs strategy and activities which your organisation should undertake for Government Bills and for Committee Bills would generally be very similar, as the same legislative processes and procedures will apply to both types of Bill.

Pre-legislative Consultation

Many of the Bills considered in the Scottish Parliament have been introduced after the Scottish Government or other bodies such as the Scottish Law Commission have first undertaken an extensive public consultation process on its policy proposals. In this context, at the end of the consultation process the Scottish Government will analyse the responses it received to the consultation, and then introduce legislation as appropriate. Sometimes the consultation will focus on proposals for legislation, while with others you might be asked to comment upon a draft Bill. With the latter, you will get an opportunity to consider the

Scottish Government's direction of legislative travel, and to examine, and comment on, the specific provisions contained in the draft Bill.

Where legislation has been introduced after a consultation your organisation should refer back to your original response to the consultation, and analyse how many of the issues and concerns your organisation initially raised have been addressed in the legislation, and how many remain outstanding. These unresolved issues and concerns will play a major role in shaping your organisation's response to the Bill.

During the consultation process you should, if your organisation has particular issues and concerns, request a meeting with the relevant Minister or Bill team (the civil servants responsible for the bill). Such an approach would be particularly effective if the Scottish Government has produced a draft Bill, and your organisation has specific amendments, i.e. changes you would like to see made to the proposed legislation.

Organisations across different sectors need to make more of the pre-legislative consultation stage, especially where the Government has a tight hold on the legislature, for example because it is a majority government. In this situation, it will be difficult, if not almost impossible, to try and secure victories on Divisions, i.e. votes, on amendments within many of the committees or by the whole Parliament at Stage 3 of a parliamentary Bill, so early engagement with the Scottish Government about its legislative proposals is highly advisable. It is at this stage that Scottish Ministers might welcome opportunities to engage with organisations which are willing to work with them to try and improve the legislation with practical, well thought out amendments before the Bill is formally introduced in the Scottish Parliament.

The introduction of a Bill

The introduction of a Bill in the Scottish Parliament is generally a formality. The introduction will, however, often give your organisation its first chance to look at the Scottish Government's legislative proposals, unless of course the final version of the Bill as introduced is largely the same as a draft Bill which the Scottish Government had previously consulted upon.

Your organisation should familiarise itself with the provisions of any legislation likely to impact upon your work, or on those on whose behalf you work. Apart from looking at the Bill itself, your organisation should also consider the Scottish Government documents which have accompanied the introduction of the Bill. The main accompanying documentation for Government Bills are the Explanatory Notes, a Financial Memorandum, a statement on legislative competence and a Policy Memorandum. The Scottish Government will often introduce impact assessments for new legislation, including Business and Regulatory Impact Assessments where the legislation makes policy changes that may impact upon business and upon the community and voluntary sector.

The Explanatory Notes provide an overview of the Bill, and also provide an explanation of and commentary on its provisions, while the Financial Memorandum confirms the estimated cost of the legislation to the Scottish Government, to local authorities and to other bodies and individuals. The Financial Memorandum will often be a good source of information about the likely impact of the Bill upon your organisation, on your sector and upon those it works for. This could be particularly helpful where the focus of your organisation's campaign is on the costs and resources required to implement the legislation, or to implement specific provisions within the legislation. This is likely to be an important consideration for organisations where the legislation is expected to place, either directly or indirectly, a financial burden on the organisations, or on the sector or sectors in which they operate or on those on whose behalf they work.

The Policy Memorandum should also not be overlooked, as this will provide your organisation with useful background information. This document outlines the proposed legislation's policy objectives, and also includes an analysis of the likely effects of the Bill on, for example, equal opportunities, human rights, island communities, local government and on sustainable development. The statement on legislative competence confirms that the legislation falls within the legislative remit of the Scottish Parliament. Your organisation should use these documents to assist its analysis of the legislation, and to inform its response to the legislation.

Stage 1: written evidence

Stage 1 of the legislative process in the Scottish Parliament focuses on evidence gathering, and on the scrutiny of the general principles of the legislation. The lead committee for a Government or Committee Bill will issue a call for written evidence to be submitted to the committee. Other committees ('secondary committees') with a role in scrutinising the legislation will issue similar calls for evidence as appropriate. The call for evidence will request information from interested organisations, agencies and individuals about various aspects of the legislation.

Your organisation should have picked up the committee's call for Stage 1 evidence either because of its parliamentary monitoring, or because your organisation has signed up to receive e-mail updates from the committee.

The committee will normally call for a maximum of four pages of evidence, and will usually set questions to be addressed in stakeholders' written evidence. Any organisation or agency or individual, with an interest in the legislation, can submit written evidence for the committee's Stage 1 consideration of the legislation.

Your organisation should seek to submit its evidence as early as possible. This will help to ensure that your organisation's evidence is given proper consideration by the committee for the purpose of drafting its Stage 1 report. Submitting evidence early will also maximise the length of time your evidence will feature on the committee's home web page. This will be useful in terms of raising your organisation's profile with MSPs of all parties.

Apart from submitting your evidence to the clerks to the committee, which is the normal route for submitting written evidence, you should also write to the Convenor and to the Vice-Convenor of the committee, along with the other members of the committee, attaching a copy of your organisation's evidence, and highlighting your main issues and concerns. In addition, you should try and arrange meetings with individual members of the committee and their staff to brief them about your organisation's key issues and concerns. This will help to increase the likelihood that the key issues and concerns your organisation has highlighted in its Stage 1 evidence are given prominence within the committee's Stage 1 Report.

When submitting Stage 1 written evidence your organisation should also give consideration to developing a media strategy to capitalise on any media opportunities which might be available to publicise the issues you wish to raise. Offering case studies to the media of how the proposed legislation will impact upon your organisation, the sector in which it operates and upon its customers or those it works for is one avenue definitely worth pursuing at this stage. If handled skilfully, your organisation might be able to generate more publicity for the issues you are raising than the committee itself when it launches its final report at the end of Stage 1 on the general principles of the Bill.

To make your evidence as persuasive as possible, you should stick to the page limit set by the committee (normally four pages), and make sure that you answer the questions set by the committee. You should also make sure that the issues and concerns raised in your evidence are backed up with robust evidence which will stand up to scrutiny and best practice from your business/services/projects. Where possible you should try and illustrate key themes and issues with short, bullet point case studies. These will help to put the issues you are raising in perspective for the MSPs on the committee.

Stage 1: oral evidence

As part of the committee's Stage 1 consideration of a Bill, your organisation should also be seeking to give oral evidence to the committee. These evidence sessions are often high profile, and are widely reported. To be invited to give evidence, however, is not always easy. From experience you need to make your written evidence as persuasive and perceptive as possible to increase your chances of being invited to give oral evidence. You also need to engage with the Convenor and other members of the committee at an early stage, and with the senior clerks, to make the case for your organisation being invited to give oral evidence.

The type of factors your organisation should emphasise in this respect are the strong interface between its work and the legislation, including the best practice and success of your service delivery and projects. Other factors which could prove influential are your organisation's track record of campaigning on, and expertise in, particular areas of policy and service delivery, and being able to draw upon significant research and evaluations of your work. Your organisation will also improve its chances of being asked to give oral evidence if its evidence has identified significant areas of the legislation which you believe should be improved or amended, and you have provided a strong critique of why these changes are necessary.

If the committee invites your organisation to give oral evidence, your organisation should choose someone with sufficient seniority to speak with authority, and who is able to give evidence on both policy issues and from the service delivery/corporate perspective.

Some organisations decline the opportunity to give oral evidence, and do so for a variety of reasons. Careful thought should, however, be given before going down that route, as declining such an invite could open up a major influencing opportunity for another organisation with views/perspectives at odds with those of your organisation. This is not without its risks, as it has been known for organisations declining such invites to then see other organisations stepping in and the committee and Scottish Ministers accepting the latter's policy positions on key issues and questions. This has made it subsequently difficult for the 'declining' organisation to 'correct' the policy context set by the rival organisation, and to influence the policy debate on these issues going forward.

Stage 1: Reporting Groups

As part of the Stage 1 evidence gathering process, committees will often send Reporting Groups of members to visit businesses, projects and services relevant to their scrutiny of the legislation. Such visits offer opportunities for the committee to find out more about how proposed legislation will impact upon a particular industry, sector or group or groups of people, and to hear directly from some of those likely to be affected. These visits can also provide the committee members with invaluable insights into how the legislation will work in practice, and to find out more about any concerns expressed by affected groups.

Your organisation's response to a Bill should include early contact with the committee to invite it to send a Reporting Group to one of your businesses, projects or services. In this respect, it is advised that you contact the senior committee clerk to explore the possibilities for a Reporting Group to visit one of your businesses, projects or services as soon as the legislation has been announced.

Such visits can be high profile, and hosting one would enable your organisation and those you work for to engage directly with the committee about how the legislation will impact nationally, as well as upon your organisation and those on whose behalf it works. Visits from Reporting Groups can also potentially offer media opportunities at both national and local levels, including social media opportunities, to raise the profile of your organisation and its policy and campaign issues.

If the committee does agree to send a Reporting Group, your organisation needs to take a view on how best to make the most of this important opportunity. Careful thought should be given to the proposed structure and programme for the visit. You also need to consider which staff, services users or customers and partner organisations you want and need to have present, and how your organisation can best promote engagement with the committee members.

The Reporting Group will want to ask your staff and, as appropriate, service users or customers or partner organisations about how the legislation will affect them, and about any issues or concerns they have around the legislation. Senior managers should, therefore, work with staff and service users to prepare for the visit, and to ensure that the latter feel confident about engaging with members of the Reporting Group and have an appreciation of what to expect. In this respect, consideration should be given to rehearsing answers with staff to the type of questions which are likely to arise during the Reporting Group's visit.

Securing a Reporting Group visit will also be featured in the committee's Stage 1 Inquiry Report, and Committee reports will sometimes include a short report about the visit as an annex to the main report. This will be helpful in raising your organisation's profile, and in highlighting with a wider audience the issues you wish to raise.

Stage 1 Report

Once the committee has gathered the evidence for its Stage 1 consideration of the legislation, the MSPs and clerking team will start the process of drafting the committee's final report on the general principles of the Bill. If your organisation has made its written evidence as convincing as possible, and you have been assiduous in contacting members of the committee and the clerking team to discuss your organisation's key issues and concerns, you will have maximised the chances of your evidence being featured prominently in the Stage 1 Report. Ensuring your organisation gets called to give oral evidence, and securing a visit from a Reporting Group, will also help in this regard.

The Scottish Parliament's Guidance on Public Bills confirms the committee's Stage 1 Report will normally include a recommendation that the Scottish Parliament accepts or rejects the Bill.[2] After the committee has launched its Stage 1 Report, the Scottish Government will usually publish its response to the report. The Scottish Parliament will then allocate time for the Stage 1 Report to be debated by the Scottish Parliament. The Stage 1 debate will focus on the general principles of the Bill, and MSPs will be invited to vote on whether or not they accept the Bill. If the general principles of the Bill are accepted, the Bill will then proceed to its Stage 2 consideration.

This debate will give your organisation a further opportunity to engage with MSPs on a cross-party basis about any residual issues and concerns you may have about the legislation. It is strongly advised that you draft a briefing paper based on your evidence and updated to reflect the Stage 1 Report and the Scottish Government's response, and circulate it to key policy makers.

In this respect, you should ensure that you send a copy of your briefing paper to the relevant Scottish Ministers and civil servants, to the members of the committee and to MSPs who have expressed, or are likely to express, an interest in the issues you are raising.

For organisations keen to try and amend the legislation at Stage 2 of the Bill, the debate will also provide useful insights into which MSPs are supportive of the issues you are seeking to raise. In addition, the debate should help to identify any areas where there might be possibilities of building up the cross-party alliances which are going to be so important going forward if you are to secure concessions from the Scottish Government on the legislation.

As indicated above, where a piece of legislation receives the support of the Scottish Parliament at Stage 1, it will then proceed to Stage 2 which will focus on consideration of amendments to the Bill. If the Scottish Parliament refuses to agree to the general principles of the Bill and to the accompanying financial resolution at Stage 1, the legislation fails.

---

2. Scottish Parliament, Guidance on Public Bills, Session 5 Edition (Version 1, June 2016).

Top Tip 8
Invite Scottish Parliament committees to send Reporting Groups to your organisation to find out more about its best practice and evidence base, and to help inform the committee's inquiry into issues relevant to your organisation, or the committee's consideration of legislation impacting upon your organisation.

9

Engaging with the Legislative Process: Stage 2, Stage 3 and Beyond

Taking stock after Stage 1

The starting point for how your organisation should respond to a Bill in the Scottish Parliament at Stage 2 and beyond should be revisiting its initial response to the legislation.

In this respect, if your organisation is fundamentally opposed to a piece of legislation in principle, then you should focus on raising public awareness about your organisation's concerns, and about why your organisation cannot support the legislation. Your organisation should also engage with the Scottish Government and with MSPs before the Stage 1 debate on the general principles of the Bill, and focus your activities on encouraging MSPs to vote against the Bill. Should that approach prove unsuccessful, then trying to improve the Bill is probably something that your organisation would not want to consider, or to support, in principle if it is fundamentally against the legislation. This point is made not as a criticism of organisations which take such a fundamental stance, but is made purely to try to help your organisation to identify at which stage in the legislative process you need to concentrate your resources if you are to block/influence the legislation.

If, on the other hand, your organisation generally supports the legislation but has some concerns about the legislation, and is committed to trying to improve the Bill by securing significant amendments to the legislation, you would be advised to review your public affairs strategy after Stage 1 and to take stock of what has worked, and what has been less effective in your response to the legislation.

After the completion of Stage 1, it is vital that your organisation should look very closely at the Scottish Parliament's Official Report of the debate on the lead committee's Stage 1 Report on the legislation. You should check to see, for example, if your organisation and its policy positions were referred to during the debate, and identify which MSPs, along with any organisations mentioned in the debate, were supportive or hostile to the issues raised on behalf of your organisation.

The Official Report for this debate will be invaluable for a number of reasons. Firstly, it will give your organisation an insight into the Scottish Government's policy positions on different issues raised by the legislation, and into the legislative direction of travel. It will also identify many of the battle lines along which the key debates will be fought within the committee during the Stage 2 proceedings of the legislation. The Stage 1 debate should also give you an indication of whether or not there are any areas where there is potential cross-party support for amendments to the legislation, and which could lead to the Scottish Government making concessions in response to these amendments. Furthermore, the Stage 1 debate will enable you to identify areas within the legislation of particular interest to individual members of the committee, and what issues they are likely to raise. This intelligence will be vital in helping your organisation to develop and progress its public affairs strategy and activities for Stage 2 of the Bill, and beyond. It is strongly recommended that your organisation's strategy includes, where appropriate, identifying and progressing amendments to try and influence legislation relevant to your organisation and its work.

What do we mean by amendments?

While the private sector has been well served by organisations such as the Law Society of Scotland in responding to legislation, the limited impact of other sectors such as the community and voluntary sector in this area has given the legislative process and parliamentary Bills in the Scottish Parliament a certain mysterious aura within these sectors. For many organisations, however, this state of affairs is completely avoidable, and is definitely an area where stripping away the mysteries is long overdue. At its simplest, the legislative process within the Scottish Parliament are the rules and procedures which the Scottish

Parliament and MSPs must follow in their scrutiny and consideration of parliamentary legislation.

Amendments to Bills are the changes made to the text of a Bill during Stage 2 or Stage 3 of the legislative process in the Scottish Parliament. These changes are formally proposed and, if accepted, are made either because a committee has voted for the change on a 'Division', or the committee or a Scottish Government Minister has accepted the change at Stage 2 of the legislation, or the change has been agreed to by the Scottish Ministers or voted for by the whole Scottish Parliament on a Division at Stage 3. For such changes to be made in the first place, however, there needs to be an amendment to the text of the Bill lodged formally by an MSP at Stages 2 or 3 of the legislation. Amendments like many other things in life come in all shapes and sizes, and range from minor alterations to highly complex changes. Further information about amendments, and the procedures involved in their consideration, can be found in the Scottish Parliament's Guidance on Public Bills[1], which is available on the Scottish Parliament's website.

What issues should your amendments prioritise?

One of the key tasks in progressing your organisation's public affairs strategy in response to a piece of legislation will be deciding, after analysing the intelligence you have gathered from the Stage 1 debate and from your contact with Scottish Ministers and MSPs, which issues you should focus on, and prioritise. Your organisation will also need to identify which amendments you will need to draft to take these issues forward at Stage 2 of the Bill in the Scottish Parliament. Part of this process will be taking a collective view on which amendments you believe you could win, if pushed to a Division at Stage 2 of the Bill in the committee or on which amendments you believe the Scottish Government would be most willing to make concessions.

Your organisation may want other amendments lodged as 'probing' amendments. These are amendments which are deliberately not pushed to a Division by the sponsoring MSP. Probing amendments are lodged to generate debate on an issue, and to encourage the Scottish

1. Scottish Parliament, Guidance on Public Bills, Session 5 Edition (Version 1, June 2016).

Government to make a statement on the record about certain aspects of the legislation, or to clarify the Scottish Government's policy intentions in relation to specific parts/sections of the Bill. Securing this clarification can be extremely useful, and will assist government agencies, organisations and individuals to interpret the legislation after it has received Royal Assent, and becomes an Act. This will be particularly helpful in the event of any disputes or controversies which emerge about how parts of the legislation should be interpreted and/or implemented after Royal Assent[2]. Probing amendments will sometimes lead to a commitment from the Minister to bring forward a Government amendment or amendments at Stage 3, which can make them a very effective tool for securing a change to legislation.

Amendments for Stage 2 of a Bill

Organisations such as the Convention of Scottish Local Authorities and the Law Society of Scotland regularly draft amendments to legislation impacting upon the public, their members and upon their sectors. By contrast, very few community and voluntary organisations actually attempt to draft amendments to Bills in the Scottish Parliament. For many organisations in this sector their involvement ends after the completion of Stage 1 of the Bill. In effect, after they have submitted their evidence to the lead committee, and might have secured some good references in the lead committee's Stage 1 Report, their substantive involvement in trying to shape and influence the legislation ends.

However, in order to secure the changes they desire, organisations should actually be looking to shift up a couple of gears in progressing their public affairs strategy and activities after Stage 1 of the legislation. An exception would be where an organisation considers it has achieved its aims and objectives on the Bill because, for example, it has secured concessions at Stage 1 of the Bill from the Scottish Government that

---

2. Under the ruling in the case of Pepper v Hart [1992] 3 WLR 1032. In Pepper v Hart the House of Lords held that disputes over the interpretation of legislation can, in certain circumstances, be resolved by referring to statements made in Parliament by Government Ministers, or other promoters of the legislation, about their intentions; House of Commons Library, Standard Note: SN/PC/392, 'Pepper v Hart', 22 June 2005.

it will bring forward government amendments at Stages 2 or 3 of the Bill to address the issues raised by the organisation.

It is unfortunate for a number of reasons, however, where an organisation fails to secure such concessions and its involvement on a Bill, relevant to the organisation and its work, ends at Stage 1. Firstly, in many cases by the completion of Stage 1 of the Bill an organisation's public affairs campaign, and those of most other organisations involved in responding to the legislation, will often have achieved very little, if anything, tangible. Secondly, this is a huge missed opportunity because it is after the Bill enters Stage 2 that organisations can try to shape and influence the legislation. But by then most organisations will have generally ended their involvement with the legislation.

To achieve the aims of helping to influence and shape legislation, and to maximise the impact of your organisation's public affairs strategy in response to a particular piece of parliamentary legislation, your organisation should give serious consideration to how best you go about amending the legislation, including the drafting of appropriate amendments.

At Stages 2 and 3 of a Bill in the Scottish Parliament you will need amendments to progress the issues you are seeking to raise. As previously mentioned, the amendments are the 'hooks' for the debates you are trying to generate within the committee. Put simply, without these hooks you are unlikely to generate the debates you want, and issues you wish to highlight will often be overlooked, or excluded from the key debates, unless they are taken up independently by one of the committee members or by the Minister.

Drafting amendments can be as difficult or as simple as you want to make it. That is the goods news. The simple starting point is for your organisation to take a view on what it wants to achieve? Are you simply looking for a debate to get the Minister to make some statements 'on the record' in the Official Report of the proceedings, which your organisation and others can then subsequently rely on? Alternatively, are you trying to improve the legislation by having your amendment accepted by the committee and/or the Minister? Stage 2 is the appropriate stage for both of these types of amendments, and approaches. These aims are not mutually exclusive, and public affairs strategies on particular Bills will often feature amendments to achieve both these aims.

Drafting tips on amendments could take up a separate guide all by itself, so this section is limited to some basic tips to get you started. It is hoped your organisation will find these useful, regardless of which sector it operates within.

The first thing to say, particularly for any organisations which are a bit nervous about getting involved in parliamentary legislation, is that your organisation does not necessarily have to draft the amendments itself if it has issues it wishes to raise with regard to the legislation. One option would be to work with a member of the lead committee on specific issues during the pre-legislative stage and during the Stage 1 proceedings in the Scottish Parliament. In this context, you should seek to brief the MSP on the issues, and on your organisation's concerns and make the case for why you believe amendments are necessary in this area. If persuaded of the merits of your case, the MSP and/ or their staff will then draft the necessary amendments, or work with the committee clerks on suitable wording for the amendments. With this option you would provide the MSP with the supporting briefing paper and, possibly also if requested, speaking notes in support of the amendment.

This approach is sometimes followed and, if you work closely and effectively with the sponsoring MSP, can be productive.

The only drawback is that MSPs and their staff are very busy, and relying on an MSP and their staff to draft amendments on your behalf could limit the number of issues you can raise, as this will be reliant on the goodwill and capacity of the individual MSP and their staff. The latter are generally very helpful, but many work under pressure and to conflicting demands upon their time, so the option of expecting an MSP to draft your amendments has its limitations. Your organisation needs to factor this into its strategy, and consider these issues when reaching a view on how it should progress its amendments. It might be that, in these circumstances, your organisation limits itself to raising only one or two issues.

If your organisation has concerns about over-reliance on an MSP and their staff and is, in any event, eager to build up its public affairs capacity and expertise, why not try and draft your own amendments, and then seek support from a member of the committee to lodge them on your behalf? This approach has the immediate advantage of taking up less of the MSP's extremely limited time and, as such, will make it more attractive for the MSP to lodge the amendments if they think the issues have merit. This would at least give the MSP draft amendments to work on, which they can then refine with their staff or with the clerks to the committee. It would also ensure that your organisation is not limited from the outset in the number of issues it can raise with the lead committee. Furthermore, drafting your own amendments will give your organisation more control over how it attempts to try and influence the legislation.

How do you draft amendments?

To get a sense of how to draft amendments to a Bill it is advised that you first take a deep breath, and then look at the documents for Stage 2 of a current Bill (it could be the Bill you are responding to) or of a previous Bill. These are available on the 'Bills' section of the Scottish Parliament's website. This will give you an insight into the scope and format of, and rationale for, amendments, as well as into the language and style used for amendments, which you can then adapt. The key documents in this respect are the Official Report of the proceedings for individual committees (for Stage 2 Amendments) and the Official Report for Scottish Parliament Chamber Business (for Stage 3 Amendments). Delving into a Marshalled List of amendments from a current or a previous Bill would also be useful, because the Marshalled List features all of the amendments lodged to the Bill. Even the most cursory examination of these documents will show you that drafting amendments to Bills is not as mysterious a process as you might have initially thought or feared.

> The **Marshalled List** is a list of amendments proposed for a Bill which have been arranged in the order in which they will be considered and voted on in the event of a Division at Stage 2 or Stage 3. However this is not the order in which they will be debated. This is set out in a separate document called the Groupings of Amendments for Stage 2/Stage 3, which sets out how the amendments will be grouped and debated. Amendments are grouped to ensure amendments that relate to each other or the same issue are debated together, even when they are not voted on together. An amendment may have several consequential amendments which

change other parts of the Bill to ensure that if the amendment is passed the whole Bill will be brought into line with the original amendment. The group of amendments will normally be debated when the line by line scrutiny reaches the first amendment of the group – however the consequential amendments (subject to where they appear in the Bill) will sometimes be voted on for several committee meetings after the debate on the group.[3]

You will also need to make sure that the amendment falls within the general scope and purpose of the Bill, and that these permit amendments in the area you are proposing. If you are trying to add duties and responsibilities, for example, to an agency not covered by the legislation your amendments are less likely to be accepted. By contrast, an amendment to add new duties and responsibilities to an agency covered by the legislation would be accepted, providing these duties and responsibilities fall within the guidance offered by the Long Title which provides a summary of the scope and aims of the legislation. It is, therefore, important that your amendments stay within the general scope and purpose of the Bill, and are also relevant to the provisions you are seeking to amend. The final arbiter of whether or not amendments can be accepted for inclusion on the Marshalled List, or if the amendments relate to a policy area outside the scope of the legislation, is the committee Convenor at Stage 2 of the legislation and the Presiding Officer at Stage 3.

Admittedly, some amendments can be very complex and confusing, especially where the Bill includes sections amending previous legislation. That said, you should take some reassurance from the fact that drafting amendments in this context will become less and less daunting with practice (incidentally, the answer is to download the relevant section from the Act referred to in the current Bill, to draft your own change to that previous Act, and to incorporate it as an amendment to the current Bill using the same language and style as the current Bill). In most cases, however, you will be able to draft an amendment to meet your organisation's aims using fairly simple language, and some basic techniques.

Just remember, if an MSP is happy to lodge the amendment in

3. Scottish Parliament, Guidance on Public Bills, Session 5 Edition (Version 1, June 2016), Scottish Parliament's website.

principle, but the wording is not quite there, the clerks will be able to tweak the amendment to make sure it potentially fits into the Bill, and can, therefore, be accepted for inclusion on the Marshalled List. Please also remember that if the issues you are seeking to raise through your amendment strike a chord with the Minister, the latter might offer to bring forward a government amendment at Stage 3 of the Bill to address your organisation's concerns. Potentially, this would be an excellent result, particularly if the Minister offers to arrange a meeting between the Bill Team and your organisation to discuss what the promised amendment/amendments should look like, and the areas it/they will address. This would be a highly significant, tangible outcome for your organisation's public affairs strategy in response to the legislation.

If your organisation has major concerns about various aspects of a Bill, the easy way to amend the legislation, and in policy areas outside the scope of the legislation, is by simply getting amendments lodged which remove, i.e. delete, the offending paragraph, section or sub-section or schedule of the Bill. This approach will secure the debate your organisation is looking for, and also provide the committee with an opportunity to address your concerns by accepting your amendments to delete the offending paragraph, section or sub-section or schedule as appropriate. Another option would be to delete specific lines or words within the Bill in order to change the meaning and/or effects of certain provisions within the legislation.

You can also amend legislation by adding new sections or sub-sections or schedules, which will include additional provisions within the Bill. By adding new lines and words you can also change the meaning and/or effects of different provisions within the Bill. The secret is to look at the wording used within the Bill as drafted, and to ensure that the amendments you draft to achieve your aims mirror the language and style used in the current Bill. If you get some basic amendments drafted, the MSP and their staff, and the clerks will be able to make any refinements.

Influencing the committee

As indicated above, the Scottish Parliament's Stage 1 debate on a Bill is an excellent starting point for your organisation to gain some strong indications about which committee members you could approach to lodge amendments on your behalf, i.e. to change and improve the Bill. Please note that you could approach a non-committee member to lodge the amendment, and to move the amendment, i.e. to initiate the debate on that amendment, but that the non-committee member will be unable, under the procedural rules, to vote on the amendment if it is pushed to a Division, i.e. a vote. Please note that the Scottish Minister attending the proceedings will be able to respond to amendments, but will be unable, in common with the non-committee MSP sponsoring the amendments, to vote if there are any Divisions.

The disadvantage of not being able to count on the non-committee member's vote if your amendment is pushed to a Division will be far outweighed if the non-committee member is widely respected, and has proven experience and expertise in the subject area covered by the amendment you are seeking to have lodged. In this context, there is a chance that the non-committee member might be able to persuade the committee to accept the amendment, or to extract a commitment from the Minister to accept the amendment or to bring forward a similar amendment at Stage 3 of the Bill. How big a chance this is likely to be, will depend upon a number of factors, including the extent to which your organisation has been successful in its cross-party influencing of committee members in the build up to the debate on the amendments lodged on your behalf.

An important dimension of your organisation's work in this area will be contacting the relevant Minister before Stage 2 commences to find out if they would be prepared to accept the amendments lodged on your behalf. Please note that you will not always have a lot of time to make such an approach, and that you will need to be very quick off the mark if your contact is to prove positive. It is recommended that you send any correspondence by e-mail and by post, and also make sure that the Minister's Bill Team are copied in (the Scottish Government's switchboard will be able to confirm the best contact if you do not already know).

Contacting the Minister before the start of Stage 2 of the Bill will sometimes generate an offer from the Minister to discuss the issues with their Bill Team, consisting of the parliamentary counsel responsible for drafting the legislation and other senior officials. Such meetings can be very useful in getting a sense of whether or not the Scottish Government will accept any of your amendments, or if it would be open to bringing forward its own amendments to address your organisation's concerns. Do not be disheartened, however, if a Bill Team meeting does not deliver any concessions, because the Minister and the Bill Team will often want to wait until they see what support your amendments will attract, and until they have had a chance to gauge the political dynamics within the committee, before committing themselves to making any concessions.

Where the Scottish Government has a majority in the Scottish Parliament, and in many of the Scottish Parliament's committees, your organisation will need to argue persuasively and effectively in support of its amendments if these are to be accepted, or if you are to secure other concessions from the Scottish Government. Building up a cross-party alliance, which includes Government backbench MSPs, within the committee will, therefore, be vital.

In this respect, you should approach Government backbench MSP members of the committee in the first instance as the Scottish Government will potentially see an amendment lodged by one of their backbenchers as more welcome/less threatening than one lodged by an Opposition MSP. Against this background, the Scottish Government is more likely to make a concession to one of its own backbenchers, than to an Opposition MSP. That said, if the issues you are raising have merit and are cross-party, and the Opposition MSP has a proven track record on a particular issue covered by your amendment, and has worked with your organisation to try and secure cross-party support within the committee, then there might be a better chance that the committee will not divide along party political lines. This, however, cannot be guaranteed.

Your organisation might also want to consider getting as many organisations as possible to sign up in support of your amendments, and to try and generate wider public support through social media. This will help to persuade the committee members that your organisation has broad support for its amendments both within the sector in which you operate and across other sectors, and from the public, and that the issues you are raising have significant merit. Ideally, your organisation should have lobbied hard and effectively before the commencement of Stage 2 on the merits of the issues underpinning your amendments. This will help to ensure that the debate within the committee focuses on the issues, and on the strengths of your organisation's case. It will also encourage the committee to scrutinise the legislation on a cross-party basis. If you are able to secure these conditions, there is more chance that your amendments will be accepted by the committee and by the Minister.

Some observations about the Stage 2 procedure

It is important that your organisation gets its amendments lodged within the prescribed deadlines for amendments to each part of the Bill. Referring to the Scottish Parliament's Standing Orders or speaking to the clerks to the committee will help to keep you right about these deadlines (no later than three days before Stage 2 begins, or before the specific part of the Bill to which the amendment relate will take place). Ensuring your organisation meets these deadlines will maximise the time available for the Minister and their officials, and for the committee members and their staff, to consider the merits of the case your organisation is making, and to take a view on whether or not your organisation's amendment can be supported and accepted. Please also make sure your organisation uses the correct version of the Bill, particularly if you are intending to draft amendments. Once the amendment has been lodged by the sponsoring MSP your organisation should try and encourage other MSPs to add their names in support (up to four additional MSPs can add their names or five if this includes the member in charge of the Bill). Securing cross-party support, including from the Government will help to increase the chances that the amendment will be well received, and accepted, by the committee.

Before each Stage 2 committee session the clerks will publish the Marshalled List of amendments, as well as the Groupings which confirm the order in which the amendments will be debated within the committee. The Convenor and the clerks will normally put all amendments on the same issue or theme within the same grouping. Committee members are entitled to make representations to the Convenor to un-group their amendment, i.e. remove their amendment or amendments from a group to ensure it is taken as a stand alone amendment, and we would advise you to let the MSP sponsoring your amendments know if you want your amendments grouped or to be stand alone amendments which will command their own debate. The MSP can then make representations to the Convenor, but ultimately it will be up to the Convenor to decide if an amendment will be grouped with others and if so with which other amendments, or if it should feature as a stand alone amendment in its own group.

Ensuring that each of your amendments is debated separately will potentially provide your organisation with high profile debates within the committee on each of the issues you are raising. Where an amendment is part of a larger group of amendments the debate will often be much less detailed, and your organisation's issue will be debated along with a series of other issues, and could get lost in the process. The Minister's response is also likely to be less detailed if they are commenting on a group of amendments rather than on one amendment alone.

Against this background, it is generally advised to try, wherever it is appropriate, to make sure your amendments are not part of a large group including other MSPs' amendments, and to recommend to the sponsoring MSP that you want a stand alone debate on the issues you are raising. This will hopefully ensure you get a more detailed answer from the Minister, and also help to maximise any media opportunities. You should, however, offer no objection to the sponsoring MSP if the clerks propose to group a key amendment with other amendments lodged on your behalf which are consequential to this key amendment.

For each Stage 2 committee day a copy of the Marshalled List and Groupings will be published on the Scottish Parliament's website in the committee's homepage section. The Marshalled List will confirm the number allocated to each of your amendments, and you can use this number to cross-refer to where your amendments appear in the Groupings. For extra clarity, and ease of reference, you should update the briefings in support of your organisation's amendments to include the numbers given to these amendments in the Marshalled List.

The Convenor will manage the Stage 2 proceedings, and invite the sponsoring MSP to speak to the amendment in their name. The MSP will start the proceedings by introducing the amendment, and confirm if it is grouped with any other amendments. The MSP will then speak in support of Amendment X plus any other amendments lodged in their name or which they support. Once the sponsoring MSP has made their speech, they will move the amendment often with the words 'Accordingly, I Move Amendment No. X'. It will then be open for other MSPs to speak in the debate about the amendment/ the grouping in which amendment X appears. At the end of the short debate, the Minister will then be invited to respond to the issues raised in this debate. Subject to what impression the debate has made upon the Minister, the latter will either confirm they are accepting the amendment or that they will bring forward their own amendments to address the MSP's concern, or will set out the reasons why the Scottish Government cannot support and accept the proposed amendment to the Bill. If the Minister rejects the amendment it will be up to the sponsoring MSP to decide whether to withdraw the amendment, or to press it to a Division. If the sponsoring MSP wins the Division, the amendment will be incorporated into the Bill, while if the committee votes against the amendment it will be withdrawn.

Sometimes the Minister will offer a halfway house solution of meeting the sponsoring MSP and the organisations supporting the amendment to discuss the matter further, and to see if an accommodation can be reached. Such an offer would also be a very positive development, and one to be welcomed. It is a clear sign that the Government's door is slightly open on the issue, but that they need a bit more persuasion before making any concessions. This is where your organisation will need to go into overdrive to ensure that the MSP and your organisation approach any such meeting with clear arguments and robust evidence. In this context, you need to look at the Official Report of the proceedings to see what concerns the Minister expressed, and to identify the areas where the Scottish Government still need to be convinced, and to then focus your briefings and arguments on these areas.

The Minister and the civil servants will want reassurance that your proposed amendments do not have any potential unintended consequences and costs which could embarrass the Government later, or have hidden adverse consequences for particular groups or sectors cutting across the policy intentions behind the Bill. Your organisation needs to look at these issues honestly and transparently, and to provide the Minister and the officials with concrete reassurances. The main thing is that you can demonstrate to the Minister that you are dealing with the Government honestly, and that the Scottish Government will be able to work with your organisation to make practical and agreed improvements to the legislation where possible.

After the sponsoring MSP has heard the Minister's response they will either then move the amendment to a Division, or withdraw the amendment and possibly confirm that they will be seeking to return to it at Stage 3. Please note that you cannot normally revisit an issue/

amendment at Stage 3 if it has already been defeated or voted down at Stage 2. In the event of a Division, the Minister will be unable to vote, and the Convenor will have the casting vote if the Division is tied. In these circumstances the Convenor's 'casting vote' will determine if the amendment is to be accepted or rejected.

As previously mentioned, if the government has a majority in the Parliament, and in many of the parliamentary committees, this will often make it difficult for opposition MSPs to win votes. To try and compensate for this, your organisation needs to develop its cross-party lobbying of committee members for Stage 2 of the Bill, and try to build up cross-party support for the amendments lodged on your behalf. Persuading a Government MSP to lodge the amendments might help in this regard, and maximise the chances of the Minister either accepting your amendment, or of making other concessions in response to your amendment such as giving a commitment that the issues raised by your organisation will be addressed in the secondary legislation or statutory guidance accompanying the legislation.

The above procedure will be followed for the debates on each grouping of amendments for the Bill. At the end of each section the question will be put: "That section/schedule X be agreed to". Before the question is raised, the Convenor will generally provide committee members with an opportunity to raise any issues about the section/schedule which have not already been considered or considered adequately. This question is only put if there has not already been debate on an amendment to leave out the section or schedule.[4]

Stage 3

Stage 2 of the Bill will be completed when the Committee has considered and debated all of the amendments lodged to the legislation. The Bill will then be updated and reprinted to include all of the amendments made during the Stage 2 consideration of the Bill. Please make sure that for accuracy and ease of reference you use the Bill as amended at Stage 2 to draft any amendments for Stage 3. The commencement

---

4. Scottish Parliament, Guidance on Public Bills, Session 5 Edition (Version 1, June 2016), Scottish Parliament's website.

of Stage 3 will normally (except for Budget Bills and Emergency Bills) take place nine sitting days after Stage 2 has been completed.[5]

As soon as Stage 2 has been completed it is possible to lodge amendments for Stage 3. Amendments must be lodged no later than four sitting days before Stage 3 is scheduled to take place.

There are some important differences between the Stage 2 and Stage 3 consideration of a Bill in the Scottish Parliament. Stage 2 is generally taken in committee, whereas Stage 3 will be considered by the whole Parliament. Stage 2 will also provide a detailed scrutiny of the legislation, while Stage 3 tends to focus on the key issues and amendments. Furthermore, only those amendments selected for debate by the Presiding Officer will be considered at Stage 3 of the legislation.

Stage 3 of the Bill will present your organisation with a number of challenges, but if you adapt your strategy there can still be real opportunities to shape and influence the legislation. It is strongly recommended that your organisation, as soon as its amendments have been considered at Stage 2, immediately starts the process of adapting its strategy for Stage 3 of the legislation. A key area in this respect is learning from what worked, and what did not work, at Stage 2 of the legislation in terms of your organisation's public affairs strategy and activities. You also need to take stock of the debate at Stage 2 on your amendments, with particular reference to key statements made by MSPs during the debate.

Part of this process will be taking a realistic view on which amendments were rejected outright by the Minister, and those which the Minister might be prepared to accept, especially if the Scottish Government is faced with a strong enough cross-party alliance on issues which have significant external support from organisations in different sectors and from the general public. Once you have assessed which amendments are most likely to succeed, you need to start your influencing work as a matter of urgency because there is usually little time between Stages 2 and 3 of a Bill.

When you have identified the amendments you wish to revisit at Stage 3, and have secured the agreement of the sponsoring MSP, or of another MSP, to lodge these amendments, you need to then consider how best to secure cross-party support for your amendments at Stage

---

5. Scottish Parliament, Guidance on Public Bills, Session 5 Edition (Version 1, June 2016), Scottish Parliament's website.

3. The important thing to bear in mind about Stage 3 is that it takes place in the Chamber, and that all MSPs are able to vote. For those MSPs who were not members of the committee dealing with the Bill at Stage 2, this will often be the first time that many of them will have had an opportunity to consider the issues raised by your organisation's specific amendments. The secret is using this to your organisation's best advantage.

You also need to update your amendments by using the copy of the Bill as amended at Stage 2. This might simply be a case of inserting new page or line numbers. Alternatively, you might want to update the wording of an amendment to address and take on board any concerns expressed by the Minister or committee members at Stage 2 in order to try and maximise cross-party support for the amendment at Stage 3. We would strongly advise this where the Minister and/or committee members responded to your organisation's amendment by expressing sympathy and qualified support, but took issue with some aspect of the wording of your amendment. If your organisation can live with the recommended change of wording, change it! This could be the difference between the Scottish Government accepting the amendment, or of it receiving sufficient cross-party support on a Division at Stage 3. Apart from updating the amendment, you also need to ensure that you update your briefing for Stage 3.

The Stage 3 briefing should take on board any concerns and objections expressed by the Minister and/or committee members at Stage 2, and deal with them head-on in your briefing. It will help to maximise cross-party support for your organisation's amendments if you can deal with these concerns/objections persuasively, and can back this up with robust evidence and best practice. These factors are going to be vital, particularly if the Scottish Government has a majority in the Scottish Parliament, and in many of the parliament's committees.

Once your organisation has taken stock of the Stage 2 debate on its amendment, and has made any changes to its amendment for Stage 3 and has updated the supporting briefing, we would advise you to liaise with the MSP sponsoring the amendment about co-ordinating a letter to the Minister. Your letter should address any concerns/objections expressed by the Minister at Stage 2, and seek the Government's support for your amendment.

Apart from approaching the Government, your organisation also needs to contact the Opposition parties and individual MSPs to try and maximise cross-party support for your organisation's amendments. Approaching each parties' spokespersons for the Bill, and the parties' research offices or lead researchers on the Bill, will be particularly important in this regard. You need to get your organisation's briefing widely circulated to your existing MSP contacts, and also target the committee members from Stage 2. Your organisation should also consider which MSPs, who were not on the committee, have a particular interest in the issues you are raising, and your organisation should target them as well.

In addition to getting your organisation's briefing circulated to MSPs, you need to target a series of meetings with MSPs to make sure they know about your amendments, and understand the rationale for the amendments. Apart from individual meetings with MSPs you wish to prioritise, your organisation should also consider holding a briefing event or meeting in the Scottish Parliament with interested MSPs. This could, however, be particularly challenging, given the short space of time normally available between Stage 2 and Stage 3 of the legislation.

Another option which should be actively pursued is whether or not it might be possible to secure a presentation slot at a scheduled meeting of a relevant cross-party group or groups. Providing such a presentation would be a good opportunity to increase support from MSPs, and also from across the relevant sector or sectors, for your organisation's amendments. Building up an alliance of organisations in support of your organisation's amendments will also help to secure more cross-party support for your amendments.

It is strongly advised that the more organisations which sign up to support your organisation's amendments, the better. This will demonstrate to the Scottish Government the strength of support the amendments can rely on, which will often determine its likely response to specific amendments. In this respect, showing that the amendments carry significant levels of support could lead the Government to make a more positive response. Your organisation would, therefore, be well advised to spend time seeking out partner organisations which are willing to support your amendments. Demonstrating the breadth of support for your organisation's amendments will help to increase the chances of the Scottish Government agreeing to either accept the amendments, or to make some other welcome concessions.

Another area which your organisation should not overlook is to ensure that your amendments attract a good level of media coverage, including social media, and you should pay particular importance to media opportunities for highlighting your amendments. Legislation can sometimes appear obscure, including to those on whom it will impact. This is where the use of case studies by your organisation can be particularly powerful in demonstrating the likely effects of the legislation, and of the need for the changes it is advocating for, to improve the legislation. Stage 3 will be your organisation's last chance to amend the legislation before it receives Royal Assent so you need to make the most of the opportunities presented by Stage 3. In this context, media coverage could prove significant in helping to persuade MSPs of the merits of your amendments. This, along with maximising the number of supporting organisations and securing cross-party support for your amendments, will help to increase the likelihood that the Scottish Government responds positively to your organisation's amendments.

It is also advised that you either attend the Stage 3 proceedings, or listen to the live feed on the Scottish Parliament's website. This will enable you to listen to the debate on your amendment/amendments, and to consider the Scottish Government's response. Where your organisation's Stage 3 amendments are issues of major importance and fundamental principle, and you take real issue with what the Minister has said in response or the Minister has missed the point or made a factual error, you should work with the member of the MSP's staff to text the MSP or to get a note sent into the Chamber as a matter of urgency. This will enable the sponsoring MSP to raise your concerns with the Minister, when the sponsoring MSP gets the chance at the end of the debate on your organisation's amendment to confirm how they wish to proceed, i.e. to either press the amendment to a Division or to withdraw it.

This tactic is definitely worth considering because your organisation's amendment is definitely now in the legislative 'last chance saloon'. If there are still a few minutes in which to make a decisive intervention, do not lose the opportunity as it could make a significant difference to how the Minister responds to your amendment/amendments. Failing which, if it is an opposition MSP who has sponsored your amendment or amendments, their front bench spokesperson might be able to raise your concerns in the 'Debate on motion to pass the Bill' at the end of Stage 3. If pitched well at this stage, there is always the chance that the Minister will address your concerns in the Bill or agree to address it in subordinate legislation, i.e. regulations and orders introduced through powers in the legislation after the Bill has received Royal Assent and has become an Act.

Stage 3 procedures

The Stage 3 procedures closely mirror many of the Stage 2 procedures, especially in terms of the way amendments are moved and debated. The key differences are that Stage 3 is taken in the Chamber, and that all MSPs are entitled to vote. Another important procedural difference is that at Stage 3, after all of the amendments have been debated, there is as indicated above a final section of the proceedings known as the 'Debate on motion to pass the Bill'. This is a short debate in which all of the parties' spokespersons get an opportunity to reflect on the Bill, and a final chance to raise any residual, key issues. This would be a particularly useful opportunity to refer to issues that were Divided upon at Stage 2, and which remain unresolved as far as your organisation is concerned. In this context, by way of a reminder you are unable to lodge amendments at Stage 3 which have been previously voted upon at Stage 2. You could, however, still raise the issues they relate to during the 'Debate on motion to pass the Bill' at the end of Stage 3. After Stage 3, the Bill is reviewed by the Law Officers and then after a four week period receives Royal Assent and becomes an Act of the Scottish Parliament.

Subordinate legislation

You might be forgiven for thinking that, once the Bill has received Royal Assent, there are no further opportunities to influence the legislative direction of travel on this specific legislation. One important exception to this statement is the extent to which the Act makes provision to introduce subordinate legislation (also known as delegated or secondary legislation) usually in the form of regulations, orders, rules or schemes introduced by Scottish Statutory Instruments (SSIs), and statutory guidance. In many cases legislation which has been passed will contain numerous provisions to introduce subordinate legislation, and the opportunities this presents to influence the direction of government policy should not be overlooked.

Subordinate legislation often deals with very important policy matters, but the problem is trying to keep an eye on the SSIs which introduce the regulations, orders, rules or schemes. This can be very difficult, and it is likely that many organisations are missing out on opportunities to influence significant subordinate legislation, which will impact upon their respective sectors.

The scrutiny of this subordinate legislation also presents challenges for many MSPs who are presented with highly technical regulations and orders, and will receive little feedback about the significance or otherwise of particular items of subordinate legislation. It is, therefore, suggested that you monitor the work of the Scottish Parliament's Delegated Powers and Law Reform Committee. It is also recommended that you keep in touch with the MSP who lodged your amendments, and discuss which SSIs are likely to raise issues of concern. If the MSP shares your concerns they will no doubt welcome an offer to brief them on the subordinate legislation once it has been introduced, and their office will want to keep you posted on when this is likely to be.

You can also keep an eye out in the 'Bills' section of the Business Bulletin which features copies of new SSIs. Responding to any relevant subordinate legislation will give your organisation an opportunity to raise any key issues and concerns, and to try and influence and shape significant aspects of the implementation of the primary legislation.

Legislative Consent Motions

One further area for your organisation to be mindful of is where the Scottish Government has lodged a Legislative Consent Motion (previously known as a 'Sewel Motion') in the Scottish Parliament. These are lodged where the UK Parliament is considering 'relevant provisions' which could change the law on a Devolved Matter in Scotland, or impact upon the 'legislative competence' of the Scottish Parliament or the 'Executive Competence' of the Scottish Ministers.

Under the Sewel Convention the UK Parliament cannot pass legislation including 'relevant provisions' without first obtaining the approval of the Scottish Parliament. In these circumstances the

Scottish Parliament will have to consider, and approve, a Legislative Consent Motion to allow the UK Parliament to legislate on a matter impacting upon Scotland. If the legislation in question raises concerns and issues for your organisation, you should ensure that you engage with Scottish MPs at Westminster, but also engage with MSPs prior to their considering the Legislative Consent Motion.

Top Tip 9

Organisations wishing to improve legislation must give serious thought to how they can amend the legislation at Stages 2 and 3 of the legislative process. Failure to do so, will often leave organisations without anything tangible to show for their engagement on a piece of legislation.

10

Members' Bills

Why a Member's Bill?

A legislative area that lends itself well to public affairs campaigning and which can deliver significant outcomes, while offering important media opportunities to capitalise on, including in social media, is the Member's Bill. There have been a number of high profile Members' Bills passed since the Scottish Parliament was established by the Scotland Act 1998, which have made a major contribution to our society. These include, for example, Patrick Harvie MSP's Offences (Aggravation by Prejudice) (Scotland) Act 2009, and Tricia Marwick MSP's Property Factors (Scotland) Act 2011 to name but two.

Please note that any backbench MSP is entitled to lodge a Member's Bill if they follow the appropriate procedures, and meet the criteria, for this type of legislation in the Scottish Parliament. A Member's Bill would give your organisation an opportunity to work with an individual MSP on an issue or issues of mutual concern and interest. This could give your organisation the chance to run a long term, high profile campaign to deliver major outcomes for your organisation, with potentially significant media spin-offs. Your work around a Member's Bill could be either self-contained, or part of a much wider public affairs campaign being undertaken by your organisation on a specific issue or issues.

Some background about procedure

An MSP wishing to lodge a Member's Bill must first publish an initial consultation document for the Member's Bill, setting out the proposed short title of the Bill and an explanation of the purposes of the proposed Bill. This will then lead to a public consultation on the policy objectives of the draft proposal with the consultation period normally lasting for a minimum of 12 weeks. The publication of the consultation in the Business Bulletin, and the consultation period, will be a good time to try to secure publicity for the proposal, and the launch of the consultation can be a useful media event in itself. A summary of responses to the consultation is then prepared, for the member to lodge alongside a final proposal.

The MSP then publishes a final proposal for a Member's Bill in the Scottish Parliament's Business Bulletin. The final proposal will appear in the Business Bulletin for a month. If the proposal receives support from 18 other MSPs from at least half the parties represented in the Parliamentary Bureau, and if the Scottish Government does not exercise a veto (because either the Scottish Government or the UK Government intends to introduce similar legislation), the MSP will have a right to introduce a Member's Bill to give effect to the proposal. This right must be exercised before June in the penultimate year of the parliament.[1]

Please note that the procedure for Members' Bills follow the same procedure as that for Government Bills and for Committee Bills, and will be required to complete Stage 1, Stage 2 and Stage 3 proceedings before it is passed by the Scottish Parliament and receives Royal Assent.

Some early pointers

If your organisation approaches an MSP to discuss a proposal for a Member's Bill, it is vital that you choose the right issue and subject area, and that your proposal outlines a practical, persuasive route for securing your organisation's aims around this issue. In this respect, your organisation needs to identify an issue which is likely to attract strong levels of cross-party support, and can demonstrate that your proposal is supported by robust evidence and best practice. It also needs to promote a legislative change which would deliver demonstrable benefits. These factors will help to persuade the MSP that what you are proposing is realistic, and could attract wider support within the Scottish Parliament. It also needs to be a proposal which will not

---

1. Scottish Parliament, 'About Members' Bills', Scottish Parliament website.

immediately provoke the Scottish Government's hostility, because the sponsoring MSP and your organisation will, if there is a majority government, be relying on support from members of the governing party in the Scottish Parliament if the Bill is to progress through all of its stages, and to become law.

Ultimately, your organisation is likely to be looking for the Member's Bill to, for example, deliver improved outcomes for a particular group or groups, or to make some other significant improvement within our society. To achieve this aim, you need to maximise support for the proposal adopted by the MSP and your organisation, and to minimise the risks of opposition to the same. Unfortunately, even well intentioned Members' Bills will not progress if they fail to attract sufficient levels of cross-party support.

Against this background, it is recommended that your organisation should seek an early meeting with the relevant Scottish Minister and civil servants to discuss the sponsoring MSP's proposal and to gauge their reaction. This meeting will give you a useful indication of the Scottish Government's likely response to the proposal if, and when, it is introduced in the Scottish Parliament. It will also give the MSP and your organisation an opportunity to consider how you adapt your proposal to take on board any concerns expressed by the Minister and their officials about the proposal or about aspects of the proposal. Doing so, could be the difference between the Member's Bill progressing through the Scottish Parliament and becoming law, or failing at the first hurdle.

By the same token it would also be advisable to arrange meetings with the spokespersons from the different parties with lead responsibility for the policy areas covered by the proposed Member's Bill. This will provide further intelligence about the level of support which the Member's Bill can expect, and also potentially offer some useful pointers about how the Bill could be tweaked to meet any concerns. Part of this process should be seeking meetings with members of the committee which will be dealing with the Member's Bill. Your organisation should also arrange meetings with individual MSPs whom you have good links with and/or you know are likely to be sympathetic to the issues your organisation is seeking to raise. These meetings will hopefully help to maximise support for the Member's Bill, or will give you an early indication that the proposal is unlikely to get through all of its Parliamentary stages. This would leave you with the option of working with the MSP to make the most of any media opportunities, including through the use of social media, around the Member's Bill to help raise the profile of the issues you are seeking to highlight.

Finally, advice and support from the Non-Government Bills Unit (NGBU) can be absolutely invaluable. As well as offering general advice and support to MSPs going through the process, and highlighting any issues around the detailed timetable required, the NGBU can, where resources allow, deliver much more comprehensive support even extending to support in preparing accompanying documents to the Bill (the Policy Memorandum, Explanatory Notes and Financial Memorandum), drafting briefings and accompanying the MSP when giving evidence to a Committee if required. However, the NGBU is there to support the MSP, not the supporting organisations, so encouraging the MSP to maintain close links to the NGBU is recommended.

The committee will follow the same procedures for Stage 1 of the Member's Bill as those for Stage 1 of a Bill introduced by the Scottish Government, or for a Committee Bill introduced by a committee Convenor. In this respect, you need to make sure that your written evidence is as persuasive as possible, and is supported by robust evidence and best practice. The same should be true of your oral evidence. Given your work with the sponsoring MSP, your organisation should also contact the committee to request that it sends a Reporting Group to one of your businesses, projects or services to gain further insight into the aims of the Member's Bill, and how it will impact in practice.

Progressing the Member's Bill

If the sponsoring MSP's final proposal secures enough support, they will have until June in the penultimate parliamentary session to introduce a Member's Bill. The MSP and their staff might draft the Member's Bill themselves or, alternatively, request that your organisation or a third party should do so or assist them with the drafting. The Scottish Parliament's Non-Government Bills Unit may, as previously highlighted and subject to resources, be able to assist the MSP with the drafting of the proposed Member's Bill, and any accompanying documents. If, on the other hand, you are asked to draft the Member's Bill or to assist with the drafting, what goes into the legislation will depend to a great extent on what type of organisation you work for, and your organisation's aims and objectives. These factors will influence the objectives of the Member's Bill.

To get a sense of the type of style and content of a Member's Bill, it is strongly advised that you take a look on the Scottish Parliament's website at the ways in which Members' Bills have been drafted in the current and previous parliamentary sessions. Once you have looked at a couple of examples it is recommended that you then consider how you would draft the Bill, using the same language and style as these examples. The secret is to try and keep the language and style as simple as possible, and also to make the provisions of the Bill short and straightforward. An added advantage of keeping the aims, and provisions, of the Bill simple is that this will help to maximise cross-party support for the Member's Bill. Only a small number of Members' Bills are passed in each session of the Scottish Parliament, so you will need to work with the sponsoring MSP to maximise support both within, and outside, the Scottish Parliament. This is going to be vital if the Bill is going to get through its different stages, and to receive Royal Assent and to become law.

Making the most of media opportunities, including social media, should be an important part of your organisation's efforts to support the Member's Bill. It is, therefore, strongly recommended that you work with the sponsoring MSP and their staff to agree a media strategy. This will help to raise the profile of the issues dealt with by the Member's Bill, and also to help strengthen support for the aims of the Bill within the Scottish Parliament. If the sponsoring MSP is aware that the Bill is unlikely to attract sufficient levels of support, then the importance of raising awareness of the issues around the Member's Bill to support the long term goal of securing the changes proposed by the Member's Bill will become even more important for your organisation. In this respect, it is vital that your organisation works with the sponsoring MSP to develop a long-term strategy, and to identify any media opportunities, including through the use of social media, presented by the issues you are raising.

If the Member's Bill gets through its Stage 1 consideration, the lead committee will then begin its Stage 2 consideration of amendments to the Bill. Where the parliamentary timetable is tight, the sponsoring MSP and your organisation should be looking to try and discourage MSPs from lodging any/too many amendments to the Member's

Bill. While welcoming detailed scrutiny at Stage 2, there has to be a balance struck because a surfeit of amendments could derail the Bill. If Stage 2 of the Bill gets passed without significant delay/political argument then it is simply a matter of time being found for Stage 3 of the Bill. Assuming this can be completed without any problems, the Bill will then receive Royal Assent, and become an Act of the Scottish Parliament. Your organisation should work closely with the Scottish Government, and with the sponsoring MSP, to help progress the implementation of the legislation after Royal Assent.

Top Tip 10

Members' Bills can provide a high profile focus for an organisation's public affairs campaign, and deliver significant changes to the law, as well as major policy outcomes and media opportunities.

11

Oral Questions and Written Questions

Why ask Questions? – the art of the Scottish Parliamentary Question

In developing your organisation's public affairs strategy and activities you should give serious thought to how you can utilise Oral Questions and Written Questions in the Scottish Parliament to meet the aims and objectives of your organisation, and to complement any public affairs campaigns and activities it is undertaking. This is an area which can work particularly well when you take a co-ordinated approach, and ensure that the question is supported by targeted media activities.

Questions offer the chance to raise high profile issues with MSPs, with other key policy makers, with the media and with the general public. The impact of the questions will be maximised if your organisation chooses the right subject, gets the context right and undertakes appropriate media activities to coincide with, and to support, the questions.

Oral Questions

There are a number of high profile opportunities for MSPs to ask Oral Questions, on your organisation's behalf, in the Scottish Parliament. These are General Questions, First Minister's Questions, and Themed Questions which cover Ministerial subject areas on a rotating basis. The Scottish Parliament also agreed that time will be made available for 'topical issues'. This gives MSPs an opportunity to raise the burning issues of the day with Scottish Ministers.

The first thing your organisation must do is to identify the issue you want to highlight, and to then draft an appropriate question. You need to identify the right issue, and make absolutely sure that it is a question which should be asked, and that strategically the time is right to ask the question. After all, there could be very good strategic reasons for exercising discretion, and for waiting for a more opportune moment to ask a specific question. Take a quick look at previous questions lodged, and this will give you some examples of the style and format used.

Once you have addressed these issues, you should then approach your local MSP, or an MSP with a proven track record in the policy area covered by your question, to find out if they would be prepared to lodge the question on your organisation's behalf. If the MSP agrees to lodge the question, it will appear in the Scottish Parliament's Business Bulletin in the 'Questions' section. Once the MSP has lodged your question, they will probably want you to provide a supporting briefing paper outlining the background and key issues behind the question. Please note that many MSPs would welcome such a briefing, and will rely heavily upon it.

It is also important that you suggest some supplementary questions for the MSP, because once the First Minister, or Minister as appropriate, has made their initial response to the Oral Question, the MSP asking the question will then be entitled to ask a supplementary question. You should also circulate potential supplementary questions to other MSPs who are sympathetic to the issues, and might intervene if they receive an appropriate steer in the right direction. This is often the most hard hitting part of the Oral Question process so you need to give some thought to the points you want to get across to the First Minister or Minister. The original question which appears in the Business Bulletin, particularly if it is a question for First Minister's Question Time, will often be very bland, and it is the supplementary question which will carry any intended 'bite'. If your organisation is a campaigning organisation then exerting some 'bite', and putting the Scottish Government under some pressure, might appeal to your organisation. Indeed, it might have definite advantages.

Where, however, your organisation simply wants to raise the profile of a particular issue and/or to get the Scottish Government to confirm its intentions or to make an announcement, you should work with the sponsoring MSP to make sure that the Scottish Government gets as much notice as possible about the question. You should also update the Minister and special advisers as a matter of urgency about the background to the question, and about the concerns you are raising. This will encourage the Minister to give a more detailed, positive response to the question, than they would be able or inclined to do if they are simply put on the spot. Putting the Scottish Government, and other MSPs, on 'notice' about the question will also help to generate a more effective discussion in the Chamber around the issues you are raising.

To strengthen the impact of the Oral Question you should make the question as relevant and as topical as possible to your work. You should also liaise with the MSP's office to try and maximise media opportunities prior to, and to coincide with, the question being asked. This will help to raise the profile of your organisation, and the issues you are seeking to raise. It might also encourage a public debate on the issues, which would be particularly welcome if it is an issue that has not yet received much coverage, or if it is one which has become very urgent/topical due to external political and/or policy developments.

Apart from increasing the profile of the issues, getting a formal answer from the Scottish Government could also assist your public affairs campaign or initiative. The Minister's answer will often help to clarify the Scottish Government's position on a specific issue or issues, and demonstrate the extent to which they are sympathetic or unsympathetic to the issues your organisation is raising. This will be vital intelligence going forward in terms of informing your public affairs campaign or activities. In this respect, you can build upon the Oral Question to develop your organisation's public affairs campaign and activities. As part of this process you should liaise with the sponsoring MSP to identify if there are any areas in the Minister's answer which you would like to follow up on either through a meeting with the Minister and their officials, or through correspondence to the Minister or by submitting Written Questions for answer.

Written Questions

Another activity which lends itself well to raising the profile of issues, and to generating good media coverage, is approaching your local MSP, or another MSP supportive of your organisation's work, and asking them to lodge a Written Question on your behalf about a key issue. In addition, you should trawl through, and analyse, the 'bank' of Written Answers on the Scottish Parliament's website to see if there are any relevant answers, which you can use as evidence to complement and inform your public affairs strategy and activities.

Written Questions can help to secure vital information from the Scottish Government. You could, for example, use the Written Answers received from the Scottish Government to add to the evidence base of the public affairs campaign or initiative you are undertaking. The Scottish Government's Written Answers to these questions can also lead to some useful media coverage of the issues, where the answer provided is informative and reveals significant information. It is, therefore, advised that you work closely with the sponsoring MSP to investigate the potential of getting some media coverage for the issues and/or concerns you are raising.

There is scope to lodge a number of Written Questions at the same time, and your organisation should give thought to how best you make the most of this activity. The Written Answers, particularly those which are informative and reveal new information, can be very helpful, and your organisation can use this information as evidence for years to come. It is also a relatively cheap and quick way of getting information which, might otherwise, incur the expense of a researcher or take up a lot of your organisation's staff time. Scottish Government Written Answers also have authority, and you will be able to use the information provided in a number of ways. You could, for example, use this information in briefing for debates, to support amendments to legislation, in news releases and/or articles for the media or to support your discussions with funders or investors about future funding or investment opportunities.

Once your organisation has decided what information it would like to secure, and how you are going to use it, you should waste no time in approaching an MSP, and ask them if they could lodge the Written Questions on your behalf. Written Questions are undervalued, and organisations could sometimes be smarter at spotting the opportunities for using them to their best advantage. A lot will depend upon the type of answer you get from the Minister, and how informative it is, so at the outset you need to make sure that you draft the questions concisely, and to the best effect. In this respect, your organisation's discussions with the sponsoring MSP will be invaluable.

Top Tip 11
Oral and Written parliamentary questions can potentially offer significant opportunities for organisations to raise awareness of key policy issues with policy makers, with the media and with the general public.

12

Scottish Parliamentary Debates

Debates in the Scottish Parliament

Debates in the Scottish Parliament are held in the Chamber, and MSPs are able to make short speeches in support of, or against, the motion for debate. The debates often end in votes at 'Decision Time' normally 5pm which marks the end of the day's formal business in the Scottish Parliament. These debates offer organisations excellent opportunities to raise issues of concern, to campaign for specific and/or general policy changes, to raise their profile and to highlight the best practice of their business, or projects or services. Such opportunities should not be passed up lightly.

The main types of debate in the Scottish Parliament are as follows:

- A debate on a motion lodged by the Scottish Government;
- A Scottish Government debate without a motion;
- A debate on a motion lodged by one of the Opposition parties;
- A debate on the report of a parliamentary committee's Stage 1 consideration of the general principles of a Bill;
- Debate on motion to pass a Bill at Stage 3;
- A debate on the report of a parliamentary committee's inquiry; and
- A debate on a motion lodged by an MSP (A 'Member's debate')

The motions for the debate can be accessed on the 'Future Business' section of the Scottish Parliament's website, and on the 'Today's Business' section on the day of the debate itself.

Please note that your organisation will often get very little advance notice of a Scottish Government or Opposition motion for a debate, which will put many organisations on the back foot in terms of preparing briefing papers for the debate to be sent to the Minister, to the Opposition parties' spokespersons, and to be circulated to MSPs. As previously mentioned, your organisation can give itself more time to try and get your briefing for the debate distributed to the Minister, to the Opposition parties' spokespersons and to MSPs by regularly checking the 'Motions' section of the Scottish Parliament's website. You should pay particular attention to the 'Business Motion', which outlines the proposed future business in the Scottish Parliament. This includes Parliament and committee business. Please note that the Business Motion must be approved by the Parliamentary Bureau before it is confirmed as future business in the Business Bulletin. The draft Business Motion will, however, at least give you some early warning of what debates are likely to come up. This will give you a bit more time to start the process of briefing relevant Ministers, Opposition parties' spokespersons and MSPs for the debate.

Different approaches to briefing MSPs

Developing your contacts with MSPs is another important route for getting early warning of debates. Many MSPs, once they have established regular working relationships with your own organisation and others, will ask their staff to contact you when they have received notice of a debate to see if your organisation is able to provide some briefing material for the debate.

If an MSP or their staff member does get in touch with you about the debate, this will present a number of options in terms of producing briefing for the debate. If it is your local MSP, or an MSP with strong links with your organisation, you could decide to give the MSP exclusivity, i.e. send only that MSP a briefing and work with them to raise the key issues on your behalf. With this approach it is recommended that you also send a copy of your briefing to the Minister, and to key Scottish Government officials. This will help to ensure that the Minister provides as detailed and well informed a response as possible to the MSP when they raise the issues on your behalf.

You might also consider, at the same time, widely circulating an additional, more general briefing to MSPs. Please be aware, however, that MSPs will recognise such briefings for what they are, i.e. a general briefing, and might be reluctant to make use of this type of briefing because they want to raise their own issues (often the result of receiving an 'exclusive' briefing from an organisation). In this context, the MSPs will assume your general briefing will be picked up by other MSPs so they will feel under little, if any, obligation to mention your briefing during the course of the debate. Given the time pressures of such debates, references to organisations will be at a premium.

Another option would be just to circulate the same general briefing to all MSPs, and to the relevant Minister, and to hope that some of them will pick up the issues you wish to raise in the debate. This is a rather risky strategy, because MSPs will often get inundated with briefing papers immediately before a debate. That said, if your organisation has a national public profile, and you have been campaigning on some high profile issues which are the focus of your briefing, then this approach of widely circulating a general briefing to MSPs might be sufficient to pay dividends in the debate, with MSPs queuing up to endorse your briefing and the issues it raises.

For those organisations unable to attain this enviable position, and likely to be competing with dozens of other organisations in briefing MSPs for the debate, it would be advisable to consider other options. Once you have agreed internally which issues you want to have raised in the debate, it is recommended that you divide the issues up on a targeted basis between those MSPs with a particular interest in your policy and campaign issues, and those MSPs who have a local knowledge of your organisation's work, or are aware of the best practice of your services/projects. With this approach, the former group will hopefully confirm their support for the issues you are raising, while the latter group will do so and also mention that they have, for example, visited one of your projects and that the issues you are raising are based on impressive best practice and robust evidence. To increase the chances of success with this approach, it is advised that you phone the MSPs well in advance of the debate to talk through the main issues for your organisation.

Some pointers for Scottish Government debates

Motions are regularly lodged by the Scottish Government for debates in the Scottish Parliament. These motions generally focus on areas of policy, practice and services where the Scottish Government feels confident in its performance, and is keen to share a 'good news' story, or wants to highlight an opposition party's, or the opposition parties' collective, failings and/or contradictions in their policy positions. Debates are often used by the Scottish Government to make announcements on a range of matters, including to highlight government successes, new funding arrangements, and the launch of new initiatives or strategies. The Scottish Government may also call a debate without a motion, in order to get an issue aired without putting it to a vote.

How your organisation briefs MSPs for the debate will depend upon the subject matter of the motion, and the policy and strategic areas covered by the motion. It will also depend upon your organisation's assessment and analysis in relation to specific aspects of the Scottish Government's performance in certain key policy areas. In this respect, if your organisation is generally positive about the Scottish Government's performance in the areas covered by the motion for debate, you could use the debate to raise your organisation's profile, and to highlight the best practice of your projects or services in the context of the policy issues raised by the debate. Any positive feedback extended to the Scottish Government, and shared with the Minister and/or local MSPs who support the government prior to the debate, could see your organisation being positively mentioned by the Minister and by Government backbench MSPs in the debate, and this being referenced in the Official Report of the debate. This could be useful in terms of raising your organisation's profile, and in taking advantage of media opportunities. It could also help your organisation to influence Government policy development if there is a strong synergy between the Government's policies in the area covered by the debate, and your organisation's best practice and the evidence from its business or projects or services.

If, on the other hand, your organisation is critical of the Scottish Government's performance in the areas covered by the motion, the debate will afford excellent opportunities to raise your concerns with MSPs on a cross-party basis. The approach you take here will depend upon the issues, and on factors such as whether or not the concerns raised are of national or of local significance. It will also depend upon how hard you want to push the Scottish Government. If, for example, you want to really put the Scottish Government on the spot you need to make sure that your supporting brief contains a good range of issues and questions which MSPs can utilise, and is supported by sound evidence. With this approach you will need to work hard with the Opposition parties, and to focus on those MSPs who you think would be best placed to raise the issues on your behalf. Considerations in this respect might include who will be most forensic in their approach, and who will have the best chance of winning the debate in the Chamber and of securing cross-party support for their arguments.

One important factor to bear in mind is that, even if you are being critical of the Scottish Government, you still need to operate on a cross-party basis as much as possible, and lobby all of the political parties, including the political party forming the Scottish Government. The integrity of your organisation, and of its public affairs work, demand that you avoid getting used as a political football. The most effective lobbying will be where you have put the Scottish Government under pressure, but can demonstrate you have acted in good faith and on a cross-party basis throughout. This is vital if you are to keep the focus of the debate on the issues, and not get drawn into the 'party politics' between the different parties.

Another approach which you could take if you are looking to put the Scottish Government under pressure is to work with partner organisations, and to build up an alliance of organisations to support the issues you are raising. This will help to make your collective intervention more persuasive, and also help to minimise the risks of any fall out in terms of your relationship with the Scottish Government. It might also encourage the Scottish Ministers, the Opposition parties and MSPs of all parties to look at the issues you are raising in a much more objective fashion. Furthermore, if the Scottish Government sees that there is a credible alliance behind a specific issue or issues it might be more willing to offer a Ministerial meeting after the debate to discuss the issues your organisation has raised, and/or to make some concessions.

Conversely, if you are looking to put the Scottish Government under pressure, but are seeking to take a constructive approach and to limit the risk of any long term damage to relationships, you should consider working with those MSPs with a proven track record of intervening on the issues you are raising. You should also be looking to brief the Minister, Special Adviser or Parliamentary Liaison Officer about your concerns and issues. This is vital if you want to increase the chances that the Minister will respond positively, and in an informed manner, to the MSP raising the issues on your behalf.

Opposition debates

The number of motions for debate in the Scottish Parliament is allocated between the Scottish Government and the individual Opposition parties. This allocation of motions is made in proportion to the respective representation of the Opposition parties in the Scottish Parliament.

These debates are used by the Opposition parties to try and hold the Scottish Government to account for its performance in different policy and strategic areas, or for specific actions or decisions it has taken in these or other areas. The debates will attract significant media interest if the issues are sufficiently high profile and/or controversial.

The Opposition debates will often be politically highly charged and, as with briefing strategies for Scottish Government debates, your organisation should remain vigilant that it does not get drawn into any of the 'party' politics, and becomes a 'cat's paw' for any of the political parties, including that of the Scottish Government. As above, it is advised that you brief MSPs on a cross-party basis for these debates to minimise the risks of your organisation getting sucked into party politics inadvertently (unless, of course, this is not a problem for your organisation, and is something you might even be actively seeking and for which your organisation is fully prepared to accept any adverse consequences).

Another factor to be aware of is that, because the Opposition parties' debates will be set-piece political debates where the emphasis is on political point scoring, MSPs might be much more selective in terms of the briefing they use. Briefings which feature, therefore, robust evidence illustrating some of the main arguments around the motion for debate might be particularly helpful for MSPs likely to participate in the debate.

Getting your issues raised in what will often be a highly charged political debate is not without its challenges, and it might be that you find the best option is to take a targeted approach to briefing MSPs. In this context, you would be advised to concentrate your efforts on sending a briefing to the Minister, to each of the parties' main spokespersons for the debate and to members of any relevant committees. In addition, it is recommended that you try and arrange briefing meetings with your local MSP, and with any MSPs with whom your organisation has close ties.

Ultimately, how you decide to respond to an Opposition party debate will depend upon how relevant the debate is to your organisation, its work and, if appropriate, to those on whose behalf you work. The timing for the debate will also be crucial for your organisation in reaching a view.

In this respect, where the political fire storm generated by the debate is likely to be severe, your organisation might take the view that it would be better to sit this debate out, and to wait for a less turbulent debate in which to raise key issues, and to highlight the evidence and best practice of your business or projects or services. That said, there might be very good reasons why your organisation would want to get involved in the debate, possibly because it focuses on one of your key areas. Each organisation must take a strategic view on the importance of the debate, and on the need for your organisation to be part of the debate.

Committee debates

The two main types of committee debates which your organisation should look out for are debates on Stage 1 Reports on Bills, and debates on inquiry reports. The important things here, if your organisation is to capitalise on the potential influencing opportunities presented by these debates, are to ensure that your parliamentary monitoring has identified those Bills and inquiries relevant to your organisation and its work, and that your organisation has submitted its evidence to the committee.

Where the committee is the Lead Committee for a piece of legislation, you need to keep an eye on how the committee is progressing its Stage 1 consideration of the Bill. Once the committee has taken written and oral evidence, and perhaps sent Reporting Groups to help inform its consideration of the legislation, the committee will publish its Stage 1 Report on the general principles of the legislation. The Scottish Government will publish its response to the report, and a date will then be agreed for the debate on the Stage 1 Report in a plenary session of the Scottish Parliament.

Once the committee has published its report, you should adapt and develop your Stage 1 evidence into a briefing paper, which can then be circulated to the relevant Minister and MSPs. It is strongly recommended that you make sure that, if at all possible, you do not simply cut and paste your Stage 1 evidence, as the policy debates may have moved on significantly since you initially submitted your evidence. The suggested approach is to ensure that the briefing paper, while drawing upon many of the issues raised in your original evidence as appropriate, has taken on board, and addressed, any relevant issues raised in the Stage 1 Report, and in the Scottish Government's response to this report with the most up-to-date information. After all, the MSPs will be seeking to debate the report You will, therefore, increase the chances of your briefing being widely referred to if you have drafted it with reference to the Stage 1 Report and the Scottish Government's response. It is particularly important to do so where the policy context has changed due to announcements made by the Scottish Government in its response to the Stage 1 Report.

It is strongly advised that a similar approach should be taken to preparing a briefing for a debate on a committee inquiry report. The committee's inquiries can be on a wide range of issues falling within its remit and responsibilities. Again, if your organisation has got its parliamentary monitoring right you will have had early notice of which committees have launched inquiries into which subjects, the deadlines for submitting written evidence and the options available for giving oral evidence to the committee. Developing your organisation's links with MSPs on the Lead Committee, and with the clerking team, will also give you advance warning of when the Stage 1 debate is likely to take place. You should bear this timetable in mind when developing your organisation's briefing material for the debate.

Whether or not it is a debate on a Stage 1 Report or on a committee's inquiry report, the debate will take place in the Chamber of the Scottish Parliament. This will provide your organisation with a major opportunity to brief MSPs on a cross-party basis about key issues and concerns relevant to your work. You could focus on providing a general briefing for MSPs, but it is advised that you would probably be best to concentrate your efforts on briefing those MSPs who are members of the committee. These are the MSPs who will generally attend such debates, and usually dominate the debate, so your organisation needs to make sure that you have sufficiently cultivated your ties with the committee members prior to the debate, and that you have provided them with appropriate briefing material for the debate.

Within the group of committee members you would be advised to narrow this down further to those MSPs who you know are supportive of issues your organisation raised in its evidence, and would be willing to raise further issues on your behalf from the report and/or the Scottish Government's response to the report. It is suggested that spending time seeking to brief MSPs who are fundamentally opposed to your stance on issues, and are unlikely to be sufficiently persuaded to the contrary, may prove to be of limited value. As a courtesy and to ensure your organisation takes a cross-party approach you should nevertheless ensure, at the very least, that the latter are provided with a copy of your organisation's general briefing for the debate.

As always, you should get into the habit of making sure that you send a copy of your briefing to the relevant Minister/Ministers and to their officials and to their special advisers. This is vital if you want the Minister to provide a detailed response to the issues your organisation is raising.

You should also ensure that a copy of the briefing is sent to the research/policy offices of all of the political parties based in the Scottish Parliament. This will give the researchers an opportunity to circulate your briefing to any members of their party who have expressed an interest in participating in the debate, and not just to members of the relevant committee. It is also advised that you send a copy of your initial evidence, and any subsequent briefing, to the Scottish Parliament's Information Centre (SPICE) just in case the researchers are preparing a briefing for MSPs for the debates, or a report on the Bill or relevant inquiry topic. Taking these steps will help to increase the chances of your organisation's briefing being used, and referred to, by MSPs during the debate.

These chances will, however, ultimately depend upon the subject matter of the debate, the level of political and media interest in the debate and how many organisations are providing briefing for the debate. This is not an exact science by any means, but if you want to play it safe and to ensure that your briefing is highlighted by MSPs in the debates it is advised that you take a very targeted approach, focusing on a few members of the committee and also on your local MSP or other MSPs with whom you work closely, assuming of course that the latter wish to participate in the debate. If they have still to decide, a persuasive briefing/phone call/e-mail from your organisation might persuade them to participate.

Members' debates

MSPs can lodge motions on a variety of subjects which then appear in the Scottish Parliament's Business Bulletin (a more detailed look at parliamentary motions can be found in Chapter 13 below). Once a motion has been lodged by an MSP, and appears in the Business Bulletin, other MSPs can then sign up to support the motion. Some of these motions, after appearing in the Motions Section of the Business Bulletin, go on to be debated as Members' debates. These take place at the end of the day's business in the Scottish Parliament, on Tuesdays and Wednesdays and after FMQT on Thursdays, and appear on the day's Business Programme under 'Members' Business'.

Members' debates cover a wide range of policy and strategic issues, and present significant opportunities for MSPs to raise major issues on behalf of organisations, and to highlight the organisation's best practice and achievements. In some cases the short debates will focus entirely on a specific organisation, and its work. This would be a major result in terms of raising your organisation's profile, and in getting the relevant Minister to engage with you about your work, and to address any concerns your organisation may have.

To try and secure a Member's debate you should work closely with your local MSP, or with another MSP with whom your organisation has close links, to agree on a subject matter for the debate. Once this has been agreed, you need to draft and develop an appropriate motion for the debate. When drafting the motion you should be mindful of the need to try and attract as much cross-party support as possible, and reflect this in the wording. The 'Motions' section on the Scottish Parliament's website will provide you with numerous examples of good and bad practice in this respect. As you will see it is usual to include a reference to the MSP's constituency or region in the motion.

After the motion has been lodged, you should start using your parliamentary contacts to try and get additional support by approaching more MSPs to sign up for the motion, and to persuade other MSPs to participate in the debate. The starting point for your organisation in briefing MSPs should be working with the sponsoring MSP, and on offering briefings to those MSPs who have signed up to support the motion. However, party business managers (whips) usually select which motions get debated.

Where the sponsoring MSP has chosen a motion relating to your organisation and to its work there might be issues on which you are looking for the Minister, who will respond to the debate, to either make an announcement, possibly involving some sort of concession, or to make a statement clarifying a particular issue or issues. Indeed, MSPs often lodge motions for debates in the hope that this is precisely the action which the Minister will take in their response to the debate. Where this is the case, your organisation should work very closely with the sponsoring MSP and with the Minister to make sure that the announcement/statement is as positive as possible.

Even where you are not looking for the Minister to make a significant announcement or statement, and the purpose of the debate is more about raising your organisation's profile, it is still recommended that you make sure that you have worked with the sponsoring MSP to give the Minister and their officials as much information as possible about the background to the debate, and about the issues you want the short debate to focus on. This will help to ensure that the response received from the Minister is well informed. It will also help to put and/or keep your organisation on the policy radar of the Minister and their officials and of their special advisers.

If the motion does focus on your organisation and its work you need to liaise with the sponsoring MSP and their office to make sure that you make the most of any media opportunities to highlight the debate. The level of interest in the debate from the national media will depend upon the subject matter, its general newsworthiness and the level of controversy surrounding the issues you are raising. Where the topic of the debate deals with local issues you will have major opportunities to work with the local media to maximise coverage of the debate. In cases where the topic being discussed focuses on, or could involve, the future of a business or project or service you run, such local publicity could be absolutely crucial, and prove critical in any decision making which has a bearing on the future survival of the business or project or service. You should also consider the potential for social media to promote the debate.

Where an MSP has lodged a Members' debate which does not focus on your organisation, but raises issues which are of concern and/or interest to your organisation, you should consider drafting a briefing paper for the debate. The first thing to do is to make contact with the MSP, and speak to them about the background in relation to why they have lodged the motion, and why they have lodged the motion at this particular time, if this information is not self explanatory from the motion itself. In any event, you should try and speak to the MSP about the issues they are hoping to raise in the debate, and also to find out if there are any specific areas in which they would like your organisation to provide a briefing. Subject to the response you get from the sponsoring MSP, it is recommended that you then prepare a briefing paper for all of the MSPs who have supported the motion. You can find out who these are by checking the 'Motions' section of the Scottish Parliament's website.

Members' debates are relatively short, lasting an hour, but you should not ignore their potential. They offer an opportunity for MSPs to speak positively about your organisation and its work, and to showcase your campaigns, best practice, research reports and achievements. If you have a good news story, and want to secure some profile for what you have achieved with key policy makers then using the Members' debate will be a good option for your organisation. Experience shows that it can work particularly well when the motion is lodged by your local MSP, or another MSP with whom you have close links, and the motion raises both national and local issues. It will also work well if the motion is part of a wider campaign that your organisation is running. If your organisation has never been the subject of a Members' debate, or of a recent Members' debate, you should definitely give serious consideration to promoting such a debate.

Top Tip 12

To maximise the amount of time your organisation will have to brief MSPs for debates, engage with your MSP contacts to ensure you receive early warning of any relevant forthcoming debates.

13

Parliamentary Motions

MSPs lodge Parliamentary Motions on various topics, ranging from party and personal policy and campaign priorities, and from localised issues to high profile, national and global issues. The MSPs are entitled to lodge motions on any policy or legislative area, regardless of whether or not these fall within the remit of the Scottish Parliament and of the Scottish Government, or are Reserved to the UK Parliament and to the UK Government for the purposes of the Scotland Act 1998.

You will get a sense of the sheer diversity of the motions lodged by MSPs by taking a quick look at the 'Motions' section of the Business Bulletin on the Scottish Parliament's website. Here you will see motions on Reserved Matters such as issues concerning disability discrimination, the human rights record of a specific country or issues relating to the UK Government's overseas aid programme, sitting alongside motions condemning aspects of Scottish Government policy and congratulatory motions from MSPs acknowledging and celebrating the success of, for example, their local football team or high school debating team.

Once an MSP has lodged a motion it will appear in the Scottish Parliament's Business Bulletin, and MSPs will be able to add their names in support of the motion. With each new version of the Business Bulletin, the addition of new MSPs who support the motion will be listed. The 'Motions' section provides a guide to how motions are listed, including their likely outcome. It is recommended that you refer to this for further information about the way motions are categorised in the Business Bulletin. As we have already seen in the previous chapter, some of these motions will go on to be debated by the Scottish Parliament, but most others will simply sit in the Business Bulletin, and have been lodged by the MSP to raise the profile of a particular issue or issues.

Persuading an MSP to lodge a motion on your behalf, as part of your organisation's public affairs strategy, should be given serious consideration. Many MSPs will be only too happy to oblige, particularly if the motion focuses on local issues or on an issue with which they have a strong connection and/or long standing interest. Getting a motion lodged can also be useful if your organisation is running a major campaign, and is looking for ways of highlighting the key issues of your campaign.

Lodging a motion about your organisation will raise its profile considerably. It will also get it on the policy radar of the Scottish Government, of the Opposition parties and of MSPs of all parties. This could be particularly useful if the campaign you are running focuses on a long-term, slow burning issue, which will require a great deal of time and effort to raise awareness of the issue amongst Scottish Ministers, the Opposition parties and amongst the general public, and to secure the changes for which you are campaigning. Getting a motion lodged on your behalf will help to ensure the issues remain on the policy radar of key policy makers, and also to keep the issues in the public eye. Your organisation needs to be mindful of such opportunities if your campaign is to achieve its stated objectives, and to deliver tangible outcomes.

Pursuing the option of a Parliamentary Motion can be particularly effective if you follow up the lodging of the motion by contacting MSPs to persuade them to support the motion. Who you approach will depend upon the nature and content of the motion, as MSPs will only rarely sign up for motions if the motion is critical of their own party, or if it cuts right across their own party's policies or stance on a specific issue. The key then is to take a targeted approach to which MSPs you approach.

You should pay particular attention to trying to get support from the Convenors, and members, of committees whose remit would include the subject matter of the motion. It is also advised that you use the network of cross-party groups, and focus on the MSP members of any cross-party groups relevant to the subject matter of your motion. Taking these steps will help to maximise support for your organisation's motion, and also raise the profile of the issues you are campaigning on and/or seeking to influence key policy makers, and which your organisation's public affairs strategy is designed to progress.

When your organisation approaches MSPs to sign up to support a motion, one important factor to bear in mind is that Ministers are subject to a self-denying ordinance. This means that Scottish Ministers generally do not sign up to support motions lodged by other MSPs. Ministers will comply with this rule even if you approach them in their role as constituency MSPs.

To try and get as many MSPs as possible to sign up to support the motion, you need to get some basic issues right from the start. The secret is to choose the correct issue, and to get the right MSP to lodge it for you. If it is not a motion which would be appropriate for your local MSP to lodge, then you need to consider other MSPs. In this respect, if you are not aware of MSPs who would support the issues you are raising, then you need to do a bit of homework. In this context, it is recommended that you focus on those MSPs who have raised the issue previously in a supportive manner, possibly in a debate or through an Oral or Written Question, or whom have been quoted in the media, or have raised the issue in social media.

Other factors you will need to consider are whether or not it is a motion which a backbencher from the governing party would be able to support, or are you seeking to raise issues that only an MSP from one of the Opposition parties would be able to support because the motion is critical of aspects of Scottish Government policy or strategy? You also need to factor in the extent to which a potential sponsoring MSP will be able to generate cross-party support. This is going to be vital if you are hoping to secure cross-party support for the motion, and to increase the number of MSPs signing up to support the motion.

One area which you must not overlook in persuading an MSP to lodge a Parliamentary Motion is putting in place a media strategy to capitalise on any opportunities presented by the motion. This is particularly important when you consider that most motions will not lead to debates in the Scottish Parliament, which underlines the need to ensure that the motion is accompanied by well thought out media activities. Indeed, knowing that your motion is unlikely to be debated will, in many cases, demand that you get your media activities in place, and secure good coverage. This is vital if you want to maximise the impact of the motion lodged on your behalf, and to ensure that it delivers the best possible outcomes.

Another area in which a Parliamentary Motion will be able to provide invaluable support to your organisation is where an MSP, generally your local MSP, has visited your organisation or one of its businesses or services or projects, and wishes to complement your organisation on its work. In this context, MSPs will often lodge a motion, after visiting a particular organisation's business, service or project, highlighting how important the work undertaken by the organisation is, how well the services are being delivered and their significant contribution to individuals' lives or to specific groups, or to the local community, or to the economy or to the country as a whole etc. This is often the start of a strong connection between the supporting MSP and the organisation and the local business or service or project, and in many cases will result in the MSP referencing the organisation in future parliamentary debates. Apart from raising the profile of your organisation and its work, the MSP's positive feedback/ support could also prove helpful to your organisation in, for example, any future discussions with local authorities and other partners about funding or about a regulatory matter. A friendly intervention, on your behalf, by the MSP in these areas could even, in some cases, mean the difference between an organisation's services closing down, or being able to continue with renewed funding.

Once an MSP has lodged a Parliamentary Motion on behalf of your organisation, they are likely to try and secure support from other MSPs using the Scottish Parliament's, and their own party's, internal communications systems. Your organisation can also play a key role in trying to maximise support for the motion by contacting MSPs to give them more background about the motion, and to ask them to add their name in support. You can do so by a combination of telephone calls and e-mails to MSPs. This is an excellent way of raising the profile of the issues the motion will focus on, and of increasing MSPs' support for the Parliamentary Motion. Social media should also be used to publicise the motion, and to encourage MSPs to support the motion.

You can also use a phone round of MSPs to maintain, and to consolidate, your organisation's existing ties with MSPs, and to establish relations with those MSPs you have not been in touch with before. The importance of these types of links cannot be underestimated, and your organisation's ability to develop good relationships with MSPs of all parties will be critical to the success of your organisation's public affairs strategy.

How your organisation contacts the MSPs' offices is vital, and you should ensure that the person making the phone calls is a good communicator, and knows their own organisation well (as they may be asked for more information) and has a sound grasp of the issues behind, and reflected in, the Parliamentary Motion. Getting these factors right will have a direct impact upon how the MSP responds to your request and, possibly also, upon your organisation's future relations with their office.

If your organisation has the time and capacity to do so, it is recommended that you contact all MSPs' offices to see if they will support the motion. It is recommended, however, that before you do so please first check with the sponsoring MSP that they are happy for you to take this approach. From experience they generally are, but as best practice it is worth checking. If the motion directly affects the constituency of a Minister, you might also consider contacting the offices of MSPs who are Ministers because, although they will be unable to support the motion because of their Ministerial role, it is no bad thing that they are aware the motion has been lodged, and has secured cross-party support. Who knows, this could even help to encourage a policy shift at their end!

Phoning round MSPs' offices will put you in touch with MSPs' staff who can also make an important contribution to progressing your organisation's public affairs strategy. The type of staff employed varies from MSP to MSP. A typical office at Holyrood might include, for example, a PA and a researcher, who will often also work in the MSP's constituency office. With each phone call you will build up your organisation's picture of which MSPs will support the motion, increase your understanding of their policy interests but also increase your organisation's knowledge of the contact details of their staff.

This is vital going forward, as it will make it easier for your organisation to engage with the individual MSPs once you know who works for them, and have built up good relations with their staff members. MSPs' staff are generally a very helpful group of people, and developing good contacts with them can potentially deliver significant benefits for your organisation. They are 'gate-keepers' and can potentially smooth or block your access to their boss. You should be mindful of this, and should use your opportunities to communicate with them to the best effect. You need to convince them that you are offering the MSP an opportunity which is well thought out, and is mutually beneficial.

In this respect, your organisation should pay particular attention to building up its contacts with the staff employed by your local MSP and with the staff employed by the Regional List MSPs for your area. These are the MSPs whom your organisation is most likely to have contact with, along with the MSP members of the committees and cross-party groups which are covering those policy and strategy areas which your organisation is most involved in, and that are most relevant to its work. Against this background, you are looking for these MSPs not only to sign up to support the motion, but also to develop good relations with your organisation which will encourage the MSPs to support your organisation's policy and public affairs activities in the future.

Top Tip 13
Where an MSP visits your organisation, make sure they lodge a motion in the Scottish Parliament highlighting the success and best practice of your organisation.

14

Public Petitions to the Scottish Parliament

The potential of Public Petitions

The Scottish Parliament prides itself upon its openness and accessibility, and one of its innovations is that members of the public, agencies and organisations can all submit petitions to the Scottish Parliament's Public Petitions Committee on key issues for its consideration. Engaging with the Scottish Parliament's Public Petitions Committee can offer your organisation significant opportunities to influence the Scottish Government, the Opposition parties, individual MSPs and other key policy makers, as well as the general public, and to progress its public affairs strategy. The potential offered by petitions can be illustrated by the success of Barnardo's Scotland's petition on tackling child sexual exploitation, which led to the Public Petitions Committee agreeing to hold an inquiry on this issue. Following the inquiry the Scottish Government agreed to introduce new measures to tackle child sexual exploitation.

Procedures and practice

Petitions are submitted to the Scottish Parliament's Public Petitions Committee, which will determine whether or not the petition is admissible and, if so, what action should be taken in response to the petition. If you would like more information about the processes used by the Public Petitions Committee in deciding whether or not a petition is admissible, it is recommended that you take a look at the Scottish Parliament leaflet, 'How to submit a Public Petition', which is available on the Scottish Parliament's website.

The remit of the Public Petitions Committee includes holding the Scottish Government to account, but it cannot require other agencies, including health boards and local authorities, to take action in response to a petition it has considered. The petition can be about any Devolved matter, and any policy issues, falling within the remit of the Scottish Government, and of the Scottish Parliament.

Petitions can be submitted by individual members of the public or individuals acting on behalf of agencies and organisations wishing to raise specific issues. Upon receipt of the petition, the Public Petitions Committee has the option to invite the petitioner to attend a meeting of the committee, and to give oral evidence. Once the petition has been lodged, the Public Petitions Committee must decide what action should be taken. The Public Petitions Committee can, for example, rule that no further action is required or alternatively call on the Scottish Parliament to debate the issues raised by the petition, or refer it to the relevant subject committee for further investigation.

Factors to be considered in progressing a Petition

Petitions offer a useful route for organisations to raise their profile, and the profile of any issues on which the organisations are campaigning or have an interest. They can also be used to draw attention to areas of the law which require amending or updating, as well as highlighting areas where there is a case for introducing new legislation. Apart from helping to shape and influence parliamentary legislation, petitions can also help to generate and encourage parliamentary debate, and to raise public awareness, on a wide range of issues.

If your organisation wants to pursue the option of lodging a Public Petition, it is recommended that you look at the Public Petitions Committee's website homepage to get a sense of the type of petitions which have already been submitted. This will enable your organisation to check which petitions have already been lodged, and the issues they have raised, and help to minimise the risks of duplication. This is an important consideration because the MSPs on the Public Petitions Committee are more likely to respond positively to your organisation's petition if it raises issues which are new, or have not, to date, had a high profile. In addition, checking out the petitions lodged on the Public Petitions Committee's website will give your organisation an insight into the varying styles, format and language used in petitions deemed admissible by the Public Petitions Committee. This is likely to prove invaluable in assisting your organisation to draft its own petition for the Public Petitions Committee.

How your organisation approaches a Public Petition will depend upon the outcomes you are hoping it will achieve. Are you, for example, submitting the petition as part of a national or local campaign your organisation is launching, and are looking to raise the profile of your campaign with key policy makers? Or have you identified an area of the law which requires amendment or updating, or the introduction of new legislation, and you are using the petition to make this call? Possibly, you are looking to submit the petition for a combination of all of these reasons.

As with most of the public affairs activities described in this guide, the key thing is to focus on the right issue or issues from the outset. When doing so your organisation should remember that how the Scottish Parliament deals with Public Petitions is an important and unique area of its activities. The policy agenda for the Public Petitions Committee is set by the Public Petitions Committee members and by the petitioners, comprising members of the public and the petitioner organisations and agencies. The Public Petitions Committee, by its very role and nature, is independent, and is less susceptible to the pressures of the Scottish Government's policy and legislative agenda than the subject committees, particularly if the latter have a government majority. These factors will give your organisation significant freedom and leeway in choosing appropriate issues and subject matter for a petition.

Against this background, a major consideration in choosing the issue and subject matter for your petition will be the extent to which these are backed up, and underpinned, by robust evidence and best practice. This is essential if you are looking to the members of the Public Petitions Committee to take further action in response to your petition, such as referring your petition to the relevant Scottish Parliament subject committee for further investigation. Remember, the Public Petitions Committee receives thousands of petitions. You, therefore, need to make sure that your organisation's petition is well thought out, and will stand up to parliamentary scrutiny. Basing your petition on strong evidence, first hand experience and proven best practice will help to give your petition a head start, and increase its chances of standing out for the right reasons. In this respect, you should also give careful consideration to the content of the written evidence you submit to the Public Petitions Committee in support of your petition. Providing persuasive written evidence, including proven best practice, will get the members of the committee interested in the issues you are raising, and will hopefully lead to a positive response from the Public Petitions Committee.

If your petition has raised new issues, or has presented issues which have secured interest from the Public Petitions Committee, it is possible that the Public Petitions Committee, it will invite your organisation to give oral evidence at one of its sessions. This will be an important opportunity for your organisation, and one which you will need to use to its maximum advantage if you are to persuade the Public Petitions Committee to give a positive response to your petition. It is strongly recommended that the person giving evidence on behalf of your organisation is a good communicator, and has a strong grasp of the issues being raised in your petition as well as of the underlying evidence base and best practice.

Prior to your spokesperson giving evidence to the Public Petitions Committee, you should work with them, along with other colleagues, to agree the key themes and issues on which the spokesperson's evidence will focus. As part of this process, you should look again at the written evidence you submitted in support of your organisation's petition, and try and anticipate the type of questions your spokesperson will get asked by the members of the committee. You can then support your spokesperson to rehearse their answers to the questions that MSPs might ask. Admittedly, as we have seen in previous chapters, it is not always easy to second guess what issues committees will focus on, and the questions individual MSPs will ask, during committee evidence sessions. What you can do, however, is agree as an organisation the main points you want to get across in your oral evidence. You should also speak to the clerks and to individual MSP members of the Public Petitions Committee to get a sense of what key issues have emerged in the Public Petitions Committee's previous discussions about your organisation's petition. This approach is not completely fool proof, but it will hopefully help to minimise the risks of your spokesperson facing a lot of policy 'curve balls', which could potentially have an adverse impact upon your petition.

The oral evidence session will put your organisation and its petition in the policy 'shop window', and you want to make a good impression which will, ultimately, elicit a positive response from the Public Petitions Committee. You need to be mindful that there is only limited time in the parliamentary calendar for both new Parliament business and for new committee business. You should also remember that the Public Petitions Committee will be acutely aware that any petition receiving a positive response will require some of this precious, unallocated time, either in the Chamber or in one of the committees. The Public Petitions Committee will, therefore, only be able to recommend further parliamentary action in a limited number of petitions, and your organisation will need to ensure that it sufficiently impresses the Public Petitions Committee both in its written and oral evidence if it is to secure parliamentary time. This is why you must use your written and oral evidence to really 'sell' the issues raised in your organisation's petition, and to demonstrate that these issues include sensible, well thought out proposals which are underpinned by robust evidence and best practice.

Apart from getting the issues right, and making your oral and written evidence as effective and as persuasive as possible, you should also work closely with the clerking team and the MSP members of the Public Petitions Committee to increase the chances that your petition will get a favourable response. The clerking team will be able to advise your organisation on the formalities for submitting a Public Petition, on the Public Petitions Committee's procedures and on the admissibility of your organisation's petition. It is also recommended that you contact the individual members of the committee to discuss your proposals for a petition. You should look at the membership of the committee, and take a view on what existing connections you have with the MSPs which you can use for your approach. Are any of the MSPs on the Public Petitions Committee, for example, your local MSP, or Regional List MSPs for any of the areas in which your organisation is based or runs businesses or delivers services, or have they supported your organisation previously in any way? Such connections would be helpful, but do not be put off if you have not had dealings with the individual members of the Public Petitions Committee before. If that is the case, it is recommended that you contact those MSPs whose policy interests are closest to your organisation.

Running your proposal for a petition past some of the MSPs on the Public Petitions Committee will provide you with useful background about how the Public Petitions Committee operates, and its current timetable for dealing with petitions. Most importantly of all, it will give you a sense of what issues have already been raised, and are currently before the Public Petitions Committee. These factors will help your organisation to build up a picture of the likely reception your petition can expect to receive from the Public Petitions Committee. Such information will influence your timing for submitting a petition, or indeed whether or not you go through with the proposal at all.

Once the petition has been lodged you should follow up with the individual members of the Public Petitions Committee by telephone and/or e-mail. Your organisation should ensure that such approaches are made on a cross-party basis. It is advised that, in making these approaches, you take steps to ensure that the relevant Scottish Government Minister and their officials and special advisers are fully up to speed with your organisation's petition. After all, it is the Minister whom, ultimately, you will need to get on board if your petition is to influence Scottish Government policy.

The general purpose of such engagement will be to give the MSPs more background about your organisation's petition, and the key issues behind it. Bringing the MSP members up to speed could have a positive impact upon the Public Petitions Committee's consideration of your petition. After all, if the MSPs already know the background and recognise the merits of the issues they are more likely to decide that the petition raises issues which should be debated by the whole parliament, or which should be referred to a subject committee for further investigation or requires some other positive response.

Discussing the petition with the MSPs and their staff informally will also help you to 'road-test' the issues, and to consider and address any concerns raised through these contacts. This will assist your organisation to sharpen its focus prior to giving evidence. These measures will help to prepare you for giving oral evidence to the committee if your organisation receives a request to do so. It will also help to ensure that any written evidence you submit in support of your petition is much more focused for having been first run by some of the MSPs.

Finally, as part of their consideration of the petition, the committee may decide to consult other organisations about the issues your petition has raised. The decision on which other bodies to contact is normally taken by the committee in open session, so you will know who is being contacted. It may be worth making contact with these bodies directly yourselves, to encourage them to make a positive and supportive response.

Media opportunities

Petitions can also generate good levels of media interest and coverage, and your organisation should put in place a Media plan, which includes the use of social media, to support the submission of the petition. This will play a vital role in increasing awareness of, and support for, the petition, and the issues it is focusing on, both within the Scottish Parliament, with other external stakeholders and with the general public. The timing of your media activity will be critical, and your organisation will need to take a view on whether or not it concentrates its media activity around the submission of the petition, or on major stages in the Public Petitions Committee's consideration of the petition as it progresses. If the subject matter of the petition is particularly newsworthy a media strategy will assist your organisation to create, and to capitalise on, media opportunities throughout the Public Petitions process.

Top Tip 14

Submitting a Public Petition to the Scottish Parliament can provide organisations with major opportunities to influence public policy and legislation.

15

Cross-Party Groups in the
Scottish Parliament

Some preliminary thoughts

Cross-Party Groups are an important part of the Holyrood landscape. Membership of Scottish Parliament Cross-Party Groups offer a wide range of opportunities for organisations to progress their public affairs strategies and activities. The membership of these groups includes MSPs, and other stakeholders such as representatives from local authorities and other public bodies, from the private sector and the community and voluntary sector as well as individuals. The main purpose of Cross-Party Groups is to provide a forum in which MSPs, organisations and private individuals can meet regularly to discuss, and to exchange information about, specific issues and policy areas in which they have a shared interest and commitment.

Some of these groups also try and agree action points at their meetings, which are then taken forward on a cross-party basis in the Scottish Parliament, or through discussions with the Scottish Government. The Cross-Party Group on Children and Young People is an example of a Cross-Party Group which has regularly adopted this approach at its meetings. For most Cross-Party Groups, however, this aspect of their work is still largely underdeveloped, and the meetings focus more instead on acting as an information exchange.

Arguably, this underdeveloped dimension of the work of Cross-Party Groups is an area which should be given urgent, and long overdue, attention by organisations across the different sectors, because the failure to develop this area is blunting the impact of many Cross-Party Groups. While recognising that Cross-Party Groups, by acting as information exchanges, can offer significant benefits to their members, these groups have the potential to deliver much, much more, particularly if the government of the day is a majority government, and has a majority in many of the Scottish Parliament's committees.

Cross-Party Groups bring together MSPs and various organisations and individuals to discuss areas of common ground and interest. These groups provide MSPs with invaluable opportunities to engage with each other, and with a range of organisations and private individuals, on different issues, and to do so outwith the usual policy straight jackets dictated by party allegiance. Meetings of Cross-Party Groups often present real opportunities to build up genuine cross-party support behind particular issues, and to follow this up with action points, which the MSPs can take forward on a cross-party basis in the Scottish Parliament, and in discussions with the Scottish Government. Such cross-party alliance have the potential, if properly developed and managed, to deliver real policy shifts and changes within the Scottish Government and within the Scottish Parliament. If your organisation is already a member of a cross-party group or groups, you should reflect on whether or not they are currently doing enough in this direction. If the cross-party group or groups your organisation is a member of is/ are not, then you should work with other like minded organisations, and with the MSP members, to see how your organisation can develop the group's role in this area.

Where your organisation is not a member of a Cross-Party Group then, if you decide to join one, you should attend meetings with the expectation that they will identify and agree action points which can be taken forward on a cross-party basis to deliver tangible outcomes for the group. If they fail to do so, then it is recommended that you look at issues which could potentially attract cross-party support, and work within the group to get these accepted collectively, and to be taken forward under a cross-party banner.

The significance of progressing policy issues and public affairs activities under a cross-party banner can be absolutely vital, particularly if the government of the day is a majority government and has majorities in many of the Scottish Parliament's committees. By persuading a cross-party group to take forward collective actions, the members will have real opportunities to engage with the Scottish Government, in the knowledge that the issues being raised have cross-party support. The key to securing such support is to focus on issues which are significant, and are underpinned by strong evidence and proven best practice as appropriate. It is also important that the issues have real merit which demand they be assessed objectively, and on a cross-party basis, on their strengths and weaknesses. The issues should also be ones which transcend party politics, and do not fundamentally cut across the political parties' respective policy positions.

Which Cross-Party Groups should your organisation join?

Cross-Party Groups in the Scottish Parliament cover a diverse range of issues and policy areas. These include Devolved policy issues and areas falling within the remit of the Scottish Parliament, as well as policy issues and areas Reserved to the UK Parliament. Membership fees are nominal. To get an insight into the type of policy subjects and themes covered by Cross-Party Groups in the Scottish Parliament, you should take a quick look at the 'Cross-Party Group' section on the Scottish Parliament's website. This section also provides information about the policies and procedures governing the operation of Cross-Party Groups in the Scottish Parliament.

Once your organisation has had a chance to review this section of the Scottish Parliament's website, you need to take a view on which Cross-Party Group or Groups it would be most appropriate for your organisation to join. Part of your organisation's internal discussion will focus on how active your organisation will be as members of a particular Cross-Party Group or Groups, and what capacity and resources it will have to invest in its membership of, and participation in, Cross-Party Groups. Does your organisation, for example, simply want to sign up as members, and to be included in the list of members on the Cross-Party Group's website because you are looking for an enhanced public profile through being associated with a particular issue or campaign? Or are you looking to be active members, playing a full role in the work of the Cross-Party Group or Groups? Alternatively, if you are members of more than one Cross-Party Group it might be that your organisation chooses to play an active role in one/some of these groups, but not in others.

This takes us on to which Cross-Party Group or Groups your organisation should join. This will depend upon a number of factors, including the type of organisation concerned, its aims and objectives and the issues your organisation campaigns on, as well as the groups and individuals on whose behalf it works. It is also important to recognise that there is often a synergy between different Cross-Party Groups, including the membership as many MSPs will be members of various Cross-Party Groups. You should also remember that some of the Cross-Party Groups[1] have a very general focus, while others are very specific and specialised. Cross-Party Groups with a general, overarching theme or focus include the Cross-Party Group on Rural Policy and the Cross-Party Group on Tourism, while more specific and specialised Cross-Party Groups include the Cross-Party Group on Visual Impairment, the Cross-Party Group on Armed Forces Veterans and the Cross-Party Group on Oil and Gas to name but a few.

Procedures and practice

Once your organisation has identified those Cross-Party Groups which it wants to join, it will be required to complete the prerequisite formalities for membership. This usually involves contacting the Convenor, or the organisation providing the secretariat support for the Cross-Party Group, to express an interest in joining the Cross-Party Group, and then paying the membership fee. If your membership is approved, the name of your organisation will then be added to the list of members on the Cross-Party Group's website, and you will be sent notification of, and agendas for, future meetings.

The frequency of meetings will depend upon how active the MSPs and organisations providing the secretariat are, and also how high profile the issues covered by the Cross-Party Group are and the interface with business in the Scottish Parliament. In this context the members of the Cross-Party Group will often be keen to have more regular meetings if their remit includes high profile business, such as legislation, being considered contemporaneously in the Scottish Parliament. When these factors all coincide Scottish Government Ministers are more likely to want to be available to provide updates at

---

1. The rules relating to setting up a Cross-Party Group can be found in the Scottish Parliament's Code of Conduct for Members of the Scottish Parliament; Scottish Parliament, The Code of Conduct for Members of the Scottish Parliament – Edition 6 Revision 1, Scottish Parliament 8 June 2016, Scottish Parliament website.

meetings of a Cross-Party Group about key business of mutual interest being progressed by the Scottish Government.

Opportunities presented by Cross-Party Groups

Attending meetings of a Cross-Party Group will give your organisation an opportunity to engage with MSPs on issues of mutual interest. It will also provide your organisation with an opportunity to network with other organisations which are active in similar areas, or share your commitments and interest in certain policy areas and issues. Cross-Party Group meetings will usually include opportunities to deliver presentations on issues and areas relevant to the Cross-Party Group. If your organisation is interested in delivering one of these presentations you should liaise with the Convenor and approach the organisation providing the secretariat to identify a suitable time slot in the schedule of meetings. From experience most member organisations will get their 'turn', but you are more likely to secure a time slot earlier if the topic of your organisation's presentation is linked to the themes agreed by the Cross-Party Group, and if there is a strong interface between your organisation's proposed presentation and high profile Scottish Government policy initiatives or legislation, and with major Scottish Parliament business.

Where your organisation is offered a presentation slot at the next meeting of the Cross-Party Group, you are likely to be allocated a 5 – 10 minute slot in which to update the meeting about aspects of your work, or about issues you are campaigning on. Such presentations will give your organisation a real chance to showcase your work, and to update MSPs and other key stakeholders about your organisation's key issues and concerns. In this respect, there are a number of things you will need to get right from the start, if the presentation is to deliver positive outcomes. The first things to decide are who will give the presentation on behalf of your organisation, what issues it will cover and how you can use your slot to the best effect and advantage.

In our experience the most effective presentations are ones which have been delivered by genuine experts, who know the subject and the issues inside out, and are comfortable to take supplementary questions and to answer them knowledgeably. Ideally, you want the person giving the presentation to have a good understanding of the policy context, and also be able, where relevant, to offer informed insights from the practice and service delivery side of things.

Other impressive presentations have been ones delivered by organisations which deliver services, and the organisations have involved service users in the presentations. This has given those attending the meeting a useful insight into the work of the organisation. In many instances this approach has helped to bring the meetings to life by illustrating the issues and themes under consideration by reference to the direct experience and insights of the service users. If your organisation does decide to pursue this particular option you will need to work with the service users to support them to develop their presentation, and to make sure that they are comfortable with this role. Taking action in this area will help to maximise the impact of their input.

If your organisation, having looked at the list of existing Cross-Party Groups, does not believe that any of the current groups capture the themes and issues you want to focus on, then you should give serious consideration to working with sympathetic MSPs to set up your own Cross-Party Group. The advantages are that this would give you a ready-made platform on which to regularly raise the key issues and themes which are most important to your own organisation. It will also give you a forum in which you can regularly engage with a range of MSPs, and other key stakeholders. If your organisation decides to provide the secretariat for the new Cross-Party Group, this will also give you significant input into the management of, and direction taken by, the group going forward.

The success of a new Cross-Party Group will depend upon the support it receives from MSPs and organisations. In this respect, you will need to consider whether or not any of your existing MSP contacts would agree to act as Convenors of the proposed Cross-Party Group, and to complete the formalities for establishing the group. You should also consider which MSPs are most sympathetic to the issues and themes which the new Cross-Party Group will focus on, and then target them to support the proposal. It is important to bear in mind that the more MSPs you get on board at an early stage, the more dynamic and vibrant the Cross-Party Group is likely to be. You should also use your networks to get as many organisations and individuals as possible to support the group. This will demonstrate to MSPs the level of backing for the issues covered by the proposed Cross-Party Group, which is likely, in turn, to have a bearing on the level of engagement the Cross-Party Group receives from MSPs.

Top Tip 15
Where your organisation is a member of a Cross-Party Group or Groups make sure the latter's meetings agree significant outcomes which can be progressed by the MSP members on a cross-party basis.

16

Parliamentary Receptions and Other Events

Parliamentary events can be an excellent way of engaging with Scottish Government Ministers, with Opposition parties' spokespersons, with MSPs of all parties, and with key parliamentary staff. These high profile events can provide your organisation with a platform on which to brief Ministers, Opposition parties' spokespersons, MSPs and parliamentary staff about your policy priorities, and about recent policy developments. You can be particularly confident of securing the attendance of a Minister, and of attracting a good turn out of MSPs and parliamentary staff, if there is a strong synergy between your event, and key business currently being considered, or forthcoming business, in the Scottish Parliament.

Key factors to consider

The Scottish Parliament regularly hosts receptions and events, both at lunchtime and in the evening, organised by various agencies and organisations. The demand for the Garden Lobby or committee rooms in the Scottish Parliament is high, which means that some receptions will have to take place in neighbouring venues such as Dynamic Earth which are still convenient for MSPs. How well attended an event will be is likely to depend upon a number of factors, including the subject matter of the event, the speakers, and the profile of the organisation holding the event. The hospitality on offer could also be a factor, particularly if an MSP is hoping to fulfil a number of commitments to attend events on the same evening.

A parliamentary reception or event will provide your organisation with opportunities to build up its existing links with the Scottish Government and the Opposition parties. It will also offer your organisation opportunities to strengthen its ties with MSPs, and to develop new links with others. If your organisation is interested in holding a reception or other event in the Scottish Parliament, the first thing to decide is the purpose of the event. Is it to celebrate a landmark birthday or anniversary for your organisation? Or are you looking to brief MSPs about a campaign you are running, or to launch a new service or business or publication against the backdrop of the Scottish Parliament? These are all occasions which would work well for a parliamentary reception. Once your organisation has agreed on the purpose of the event, you must then consider and agree the key themes on which the event will focus.

You should also take a view on which MSPs you want to attend the event. Is it a general invite, with your organisation simply wanting as many MSPs as possible to attend? Or are there particular MSPs whom you want to attend, possibly those with a proven track record on the issues under consideration? And are you keen to get MSPs from a particular party to attend, with one eye on building up a cross-party alliance behind amendments which will be voted on at Stage 2 or 3 of a piece of legislation currently going through the Scottish Parliament?

When your organisation has addressed these preliminary issues, you must then take a view on which MSP you will approach to sponsor the event. Apart from the MSP adding their prestige and backing to the event, on a more mundane level you will need to get an MSP to sponsor the event in order to book a room in the Scottish Parliament. Room bookings are free, but you will be charged for refreshments.

Careful thought should be given to which MSP you approach to sponsor the event. A lot will depend upon the type of event you are planning to stage, its subject and key themes. You could approach your local MSP to sponsor the event, and this will help to strengthen your existing relations with the MSP, or to develop relations with the MSP if you have not had much contact with them to date. Alternatively, you might want to approach an MSP who has been particularly active, and has enjoyed a high profile, on the issues/subject which the event will focus on. This could help to maximise the number of MSPs attending, depending upon the issues/subject matter that are being raised, and the profile which the MSP enjoys on the issue in question.

The type of event

You will need to consider if the event will be to celebrate some landmark occasion or achievement for your organisation, or if the event will be a reception to brief MSPs and parliamentary staff about a campaign or publication you are launching, or about your organisation's policy priorities. Once you have decided this issue, the main options for parliamentary events are either lunchtime receptions in a committee room, or an evening reception in either the Garden Lobby or in a committee room or a daytime exhibition in the designated exhibition area.

All of these types of events have advantages and disadvantages. A lunchtime reception, for example, might attract a good turnout of MSPs and parliamentary staff if you are providing lunch, and you can avoid a clash with the different political parties' regular meetings of their MSPs and key committee business. You should, however, be aware that a lunchtime event will not give you much time for the event itself as the time available for the room will be limited, so if you go for this option you should avoid getting too elaborate in your planning. You will have little time, and will need to make the most of it.

An evening reception in the Garden Lobby is a good option if you can get enough MSPs and parliamentary staff to attend. There is also the advantage of being able to attract MSPs who are literally passing through the Garden Lobby, which is the Scottish Parliament's main thoroughfare, to pop into your event. It is, however, a big space, and if you do not get the right turnout your event could end up looking like a wash-out. Maximising turnout will also depend upon which other competing events are being held that night. MSPs receive dozens of invites each day, and you need to make sure that your invite stands out if you are to persuade MSPs to drop into your event even for a short time. Similar challenges face organisations holding evening events in Scottish Parliament committee rooms. Because of the desirability of the Garden Lobby for hosting events, you will usually have to book it many months ahead. Committee rooms can be easier to book, but even here the next available slot may be some time away.

Unfortunately, there is never a perfect time for a parliamentary event, because you will always be competing with other events and MSPs' diary commitments. You could, for example, face competition from a political party's meeting which will be attended by all of the

MSPs of a particular party, or it could be that your event clashes with a parliamentary reception arranged by a private sector company or agency renowned for its lavish hospitality. What you can do is to try and give your organisation's event as much chance as possible of a good turnout of MSPs and parliamentary staff by attempting to avoid clashes of dates with some of these events. A good place to start is to liaise with the sponsoring MSP and their staff, and with the parliamentary events team. They will be able to give you some pointers about possible times and dates for your event, including those to avoid, and you can then take a view on what will work best for your organisation.

Logistics for progressing the event

Once your organisation has secured agreement from an MSP to sponsor its parliamentary reception, and you have identified a mutually convenient time and date, you will need to liaise with the MSP's staff to complete a room booking form. After this form has been completed it will be submitted by the MSP's staff to the parliamentary events team who will then confirm the booking. With the time and date agreed, and the room booking confirmed, your organisation then needs to start the process of promoting the event to maximise the turnout of MSPs and parliamentary staff. This is another area in which the MSP's staff can play an invaluable role, as they will be able to publicise the event within the Scottish Parliament, and to ensure that MSPs of all parties receive notification of the event.

Your organisation can also play a vital role in promoting the event. You should use all of your normal networks to publicise the event. In addition, you should publicise your organisation's event under the 'AOB' part of the agenda of any relevant Cross-Party Group meetings. If you are attending the political parties' conferences, and your parliamentary event will take place after the conferences, you should use the conferences to engage with as many MSPs as possible, and to let the different parties know about your event. Ideally, you should have flyers published for this very purpose, which you can then distribute to the MSPs and parliamentary staff you meet at their party's conference.

Once you have compiled your guest list you should send out a 'save the date' e-mail to all of the MSPs you are inviting, as well as to all of your other guests. This e-mail should go out at least six weeks before the event, and should confirm details of the event. You should follow this up with a formal invite letter or card invite. It is recommended that you give the MSPs at least one month's notice of the event, because of the competition from other events/commitments which will be going on. Once the invites are out, your organisation should follow up the invites with phone calls to the offices of all of the MSPs you are inviting. You should keep a running total of all of the responses you receive so that you have a clear idea of which MSPs will attend the event, those MSPs who might attend and those who will definitely not attend, and what the overall numbers of attendees will be. To ensure that the arrangements for the event are progressed as smoothly as possible, you might also want to adapt the pro forma suggested in Chapter 3 for planning a Ministerial or MSP visit.

How do you make your event stand out?

Your organisation is likely to face stiff competition from a number of events, regardless of what date and time you opt for. The main thing then is to make sure that your event stands out, and that you secure the attendance of a Scottish Government Minister, and maximise the number of MSPs and key parliamentary staff who attend the event. Promoting the event will be critical in this regard, and you should work closely with the sponsoring MSP's staff to get that right. Ensuring there is a good interface between the subject matter and issues which your event will focus on, and key business in the Scottish Parliament could also prove significant. You are more likely to secure the attendance of the Minister, and to get a good turnout of MSPs if the event is focusing on topical issues. To take an example, if your event is a briefing event about a new piece of legislation, you should try and stage the event just before the legislation is about to commence, or during its Stage 1 proceedings, in the Scottish Parliament. This will help to maximise the attendance of MSPs with an active interest in the legislation, or whom are looking to get up to speed on the legislation.

You should also give careful consideration to the structure of the event, and to which speakers you invite to provide inputs. The MSPs will want to find out more about the key issues, but they will also want an opportunity to engage interactively on these issues. The structure of the event will depend upon whether or not the event will take place at lunchtime, or evening, on a sitting day, as this will determine how much time you will have from start to finish for the event. It is recommended that for a celebration event such as an organisation's landmark anniversary you allow no more than half an hour for the formal speeches, allow some time for questions and answers and for discussion, and allocate the remainder of the time for networking. For a briefing event, or to launch a publication or campaign, you might wish to allow longer for the formal inputs.

Ensuring that you get good speakers for your event will also help to generate interest in your organisation's parliamentary event. MSPs will be particularly keen to turn up to your event if you have been able to secure inputs from speakers who are high profile and/or are recognised experts in their field, and in the areas which your event will focus on. You should invite the relevant Scottish Government Minister to give the keynote speech, especially if the event is going to focus on a new piece of legislation which they will be responsible for steering through the Scottish Parliament. To increase the chances of the Minister agreeing to participate your organisation should allow at least two to three months from sending its invite letter to the date of the event itself. Ministers receive large numbers of invites, and you need to give them as much notice as possible if your invite is to receive a positive response.

In terms of protocol it is recommended that you ask the sponsoring MSP to provide an input, and that a senior member of your organisation provides a formal welcome/introduction to the event. It is advised that you do not overload the event with speakers. Other speakers should be selected on the basis of their expertise and experience in particular areas relevant to the event. In this respect, it is also suggested that you try and get a balance of speakers, as much as possible, between those who can speak about the evidence and policy developments, and those who are able to speak from a service delivery/business or corporate perspective. You should also give serious consideration to involving service users in the event as their participation could provide invaluable insights from direct experience, and help to illustrate the main issues.

Publicising the event

Parliamentary events can be very high profile, and offer good opportunities to try and generate media interest in the issues on which your event will focus. It is, therefore, recommended that you develop a media plan, including the use of social media, to support the event, and to make the most of these opportunities. Focusing your event on highly topical issues, and/or issues where there is a strong connection with current or future business in the Scottish Parliament, will help to promote media interest in your event. A parliamentary event designed to celebrate a landmark anniversary or to launch a campaign or a new publication are also the type of initiatives likely to secure interest from the media. In many cases you will not know how much interest your event will attract amongst the media until your news release is out there, and you start getting phone calls from news desks or not, as the case might be.

Exhibitions

Another type of parliamentary event which you may want to give some thought to is holding an exhibition. The Scottish Parliament has some exhibition space, and this can be booked up by organisations if they can persuade an MSP to sponsor the event. Exhibition spaces can be booked up for a week, and they give organisations opportunities to run exhibitions about their work. The types of exhibitions which work well in this space are those involving displays of photographs, and other visual displays.

Apart from giving your organisation an opportunity to stage an exhibition, such an event will also provide chances to meet MSPs and their staff and to build up your contacts when the latter visit your exhibition space. Please note that all members of your organisation's staff working at the exhibition will need to have parliamentary security passes if they are to help out at your organisation's exhibition. This means that they will have to complete application forms for parliamentary passes. The processing of these passes involves vetting and security arrangements, which means that you will need to allow sufficient time for your staff to have their applications processed if they are to support the exhibition.

Top Tip 16

To maximise the impact of a members' debate that you have worked on with an MSP, why not combine it with a post-debate reception in one of the Parliament's committee rooms. You can then invite guests to come and watch the debate before moving on to the reception.

17

Party Conferences

All of the political parties represented in the Scottish Parliament have annual conferences, with some holding conferences in both the Spring and Autumn of each year. These conferences are significant political gatherings, and offer major opportunities to engage with Scottish Ministers, special advisers, front bench spokespersons from the different parties, MSPs, MPs, Peers, councillors, parliamentary researchers and a host of other key policy makers within each of the political parties. The party conferences will offer your organisation a platform to undertake a range of public affairs activities. Maintaining some level of presence at these conferences should, therefore, be an important part of your organisation's public affairs strategy.

Admittedly, attending the party conferences can be expensive, and your organisation will need to take a view on whether or not it can afford to be represented at all of the party conferences and, if not, which ones it should prioritise. Your organisation will also need to decide if it can afford to attend both the Spring and/or Autumn conferences of the political parties whose conferences you decide to prioritise. It will also need to consider who should represent the organisation because you will need someone experienced and senior enough to be able to talk knowledgeably about all aspects of your work, including policy, campaign issues and, as appropriate, about business and operational matters, including front-line services. You will also need someone who can act with sufficient tact and diplomacy to engage with politicians at their party's conference, given that many of the MSPs and party activists will often be more interested in their party's own internal developments and politics than in your organisation's key policy issues and themes.

The organisation will also have to decide how it wishes to manage its presence at the party conferences. Does your organisation just want to send observers? Or perhaps run a stall at an exhibition space, possibly with other like-minded organisations to reduce costs, or in your own right? Or are you looking to also hold a fringe meeting at each, or some, of the party conferences? These options all cost money, and all have advantages and disadvantages associated with them, which are considered in more detail below.

Planning and managing your organisation's presence

Once your organisation has decided which conferences it will be attending and has confirmed their location and dates, your organisation should start planning how it will manage its presence. One of the first tasks your organisation will need to complete is to make contact with the respective party headquarters, and ask those organising their party's conference to send you a copy of the conference brochure for potential exhibitors (if they have not already sent it to your organisation). You should also speak to them about costs, particularly if your organisation is minded to pay for an exhibition space and/or fringe event. In these times of financial stringency and cutbacks, remember that the political parties are also feeling the pinch and will often be struggling to sell all of the exhibition spaces and fringe event slots at their conference. So do not accept the first quote you are offered. Negotiate with the political party concerned. By doing so, your organisation could save itself hundreds of pounds across the different conferences it decides to attend.

All of the parties will require your organisation to complete security forms for all members of your staff who will be attending their conference. Some of these applications require a photo ID. Make sure that you complete the necessary forms and get them processed in plenty of time. Failure to do so could result in significant delays in your organisation being able to access the conference venue. Apart from the embarrassment factor, such delays will significantly eat into your organisation's opportunities to engage with the MSPs and other key policy makers.

Once your organisation has booked up for a particular party conference it wants to attend, it should ensure that all of your MSP contacts in that party are aware that your organisation will be attending. MSPs should be invited to meet up with your organisation's main contact for a chat, either over a coffee or by popping along to visit your exhibition space or by attending your fringe event. In addition, your organisation should contact those MSPs with whom you would like to develop ties. Give some thought to how you approach this, as personalising the approach as much as possible, will often increase the likelihood of a positive response.

Also are you contacting the MSP because your organisation already knows them as your local MSP, and it would be good to catch up with them on various issues? Or are you contacting particular MSPs because they are members of a committee which will be dealing with a piece of legislation that your organisation is seeking to shape and influence? Or are you seeking to enlist the MSP's support in advance of a tricky meeting with your funders? Some organisations just turn up without making previous arrangements to meet specific MSPs, and still manage to meet a lot of MSPs. This, however, could be a risky strategy. It is strongly advised that doing this basic legwork, well in advance of the conference, will help your organisation to maximise the number of contacts it has with Scottish Ministers, with front bench spokespersons from the opposition parties, with MSPs, and with MPs or Peers with councillors and with other key policy makers over the course of the different party conferences.

Exhibition spaces

Paying for an exhibition space can be expensive, so try and negotiate hard to get your organisation's costs down. If costs are the overriding factor in determining which conferences your organisation attends, you need to balance contacting the organisers early to try and get as good an exhibition space location as possible, with leaving it as late as possible to try and extract the best discount from the organisers if they are desperately trying to sell their remaining slots.

Exhibition spaces will give your organisation a base which will advertise your presence for the duration of the conference. It will give MSPs, local councillors and other party activists an opportunity to drop by, and to engage with you on key issues. It is their conference, and you have to bear in mind that sometimes your arrangements to meet specific MSPs will get overtaken by internal party politics or by conference developments. Having a stall maximises the chances of the MSP coming to meet you eventually; even if your initial arrangements get lost in the conference hurly burly.

Exhibition spaces usually include two delegates passes. With the agreement of the political party holding the conference, you may be able to staff your exhibition space on a rota basis if that suits your organisation, and if your organisation has the capacity to do so. This would be an option if your organisation has a business/businesses or local services in the city or town where the party conference is taking place, and you are able to draw upon the assistance of local members of staff to help out on the stall. It will greatly strengthen your conference presence if you are able to field these local 'experts' who can talk first hand, and knowledgeably about the work you are doing in local communities or across the region. You may even be able to invite a politician to briefly leave the conference and come to visit your local office or service if it is near the conference venue. It will also be valuable if there is a link between a current policy development or new piece of legislation being considered in the Scottish or UK Parliaments and your work. Giving politicians a chance to hear first hand from local colleagues about how policy development or legislation could impact upon services and service users or businesses and customers can be used to strengthen your organisation's public affairs activities in these areas.

Subject to how much you have paid for your organisation's exhibition space, you will have options to use either a large 'nomadic' banner or pop-up banners. The cost of your exhibition space package will also normally include a table, which you can use to exhibit publications and other materials which profile your organisation or issues upon which you are campaigning. You should give careful thought to what materials you exhibit, as this is what your organisation will be using to 'sell' itself at the conference and to any equipment you may need to exhibit your publications. Having experienced members of staff at the exhibition space will help your organisation to ensure that MSPs with a particular interest are given information and material to reflect their policy priorities.

It is usual at each party's conference that the organisers will arrange for Scottish Ministers or key party spokespersons and other high profile figures as appropriate to go round the exhibition space meeting all of the exhibiting organisations. This provides an opportunity to meet the politicians, and to get some photos taken which can be helpful for profiling and marketing purposes. It is also an opportunity for your organisation to speak to the politicians, and to raise issues with them or to extend an invite to visit your organisation, so make the most of it. If the organisers have not got the senior politicians around the stalls in sufficient numbers, ask them to do so. The organisers are usually highly professional, and will genuinely do their best to accommodate such requests. They also know that, in some cases, it could be the difference between your organisation attending, and not attending, their next conference.

Observers

If your organisation does not have the resources to pay for an exhibition space, or if it is not convinced of the benefits of paying for an exhibition space, at the respective party conferences, you might still want to consider purchasing observer passes to attend the party conferences you wish to prioritise. Sending observers will be a cheaper way of ensuring you have a presence at the conferences. This will work well if you have undertaken a lot of preparatory work to pre-arrange meetings with MSPs and other key contacts at the conference. You should combine this approach with 'working the room' to catch up with any contacts with whom you were unable to pre-arrange meetings beforehand.

The only disadvantages of this approach are that, without an exhibition space, you will be limited in the publications you can bring and distribute. There is also a risk that, if it is a particularly busy conference or if it is dominated by internal party politics, you might struggle to engage with as many MSPs as you would like if your pre-arranged appointments fall through or are delayed. The conference is, after all, about the political party itself, and it is an opportunity first and foremost for the members of that party to network with each other, and to develop, and to engage in, their own internal political agendas, and to contribute to their own internal political developments. In this respect, having an exhibition space gives you a guaranteed presence and, even if many of your pre-arranged meetings fall through in the face of the conference hurly burly, many of the MSPs will at some point during the conference drop by your stall. That said, some organisations have very successful conferences, and manage to engage with all of their key contacts and targets, just by sending observers. Your organisation should, therefore, choose the option which it believes will work best for it at particular conferences.

Fringe meetings

One of the most high profile public affairs activities which you can undertake at a party conference is to hold a fringe meeting either at lunchtime or in the evening. Each party conference will include dozens of these events, so you need to consider this option in the full knowledge that your fringe meeting will face stiff competition from similar events in trying to attract MSPs, MPs, Peers, local councillors and other key policy makers to attend. Fringe meetings can be very expensive, and one of the first issues which your organisation will need to decide is whether or not you hold your own fringe event, or hold a fringe event with other partners in order to reduce the costs. What you will save in costs you will need to balance against losing exclusive control over shaping and managing the event and sharing the profile from the event with other organisations.

If your organisation decides to hold a fringe event, it is likely to face high levels of competition (both direct and indirect) from other organisations, anxious to ensure that their fringe meetings attract as many MSPs and other policy makers as possible. Your organisation, therefore, needs to try and make sure your fringe event is 'the hot ticket' for that conference, or at least for the lunchtime or evening of a specific day at a particular conference. Choosing an interesting theme, and making it as topical as possible, will certainly help to make your organisation's fringe event more attractive. You also need to try and get high profile speakers, who will help to maximise the size of the audience. Securing the involvement of a Scottish Government Minister or a front bench spokesperson from an Opposition party or another national political figure will help to generate interest in your event. Securing speakers who are recognised experts in particular policy areas will also help to increase such interest.

It is advised that your organisation should be very particular about the venue you accept from the organisers for your fringe event. Over the years the different political parties have used a wide range of venues within the different conference centres. Some have been state of the art conference rooms, while other fringe events have been held in foyers or large communal areas within earshot of other events. If the organisers are unable to guarantee you certain standards, such as having a self-contained room with good acoustics, then it would be advisable for your organisation to pass on the offer. There will be plenty of other opportunities.

This advice is underlined by the recent sight of a senior politician trying to unravel the Scottish Government's thinking on a fairly complex issue at a fringe meeting, where the 'venue' was a foyer surrounded by noisy public spaces. This resulted in the unedifying spectacle of the senior politician having to bellow over the chatter from a neighbouring bar within the venue, and not being heard by many members of the audience. A lot of planning went into this event, the subjects were highly topical and the speakers were impressive on paper, but the overall effect was ruined by the poor venue.

No doubt the organisation paid a lot of money for the venue, but having assembled an excellent looking fringe event, they then nullified all of their good work by staging the event in a noisy foyer. The overall impact of this particular fringe event was poor, and the event was remembered for all of the wrong reasons – the cramped seating arrangements, and the continuous background noise drowning out the guest speakers! It would have been better if the organisation had first checked out the venue on offer within the conference, and then politely declined. They could have then used their resources to organise their own event after the party conference seasons, and at a venue where the keynote speakers would be heard and could be engaged with.

Promoting the fringe event

Once your organisation has decided in principle to hold a fringe event, it needs to decide which conferences it will focus on. Is it looking to have a fringe event at all of the party conferences, or will you limit your fringe events to one or two, possibly the governing party's own conference and the main Opposition party's conference? Having made these decisions you then need to start the process of promoting your fringe events. Before the conferences you should contact the relevant party's MSPs and other key policy makers, and let them know that you will be holding a fringe event at their party conference. Ideally, you should get flyers or invitations sent out to these groups well in advance of the conference, and follow up with targeted phone calls.

You will require an MSP to host the event, and you should liaise with their office to help your organisation to promote the event. It is advised that you involve the MSP in the event by either chairing the event, or by delivering one of the speeches. Hopefully, they will be very supportive, and use their party's internal communications to publicise the event to their colleagues. Your fringe event will also be featured in the conference programme, and you should use this to promote the event as effectively as possible. At the conference you should also distribute flyers publicising the event to Ministers and party spokespersons, to MSPs, to councillors and to other party activists as appropriate.

Remember you will be competing with many other events, and you need to make sure that the delegates know when your event will be taking place. You should also give some consideration to the type of refreshments you will provide, because this factor will influence some of the delegates in deciding whether or not to attend. Providing lunch, or light refreshments and wine for an evening reception, could make all of the difference in how many MSPs and other delegates decide to attend your event. Refreshments can be expensive, and this is where working with partners to deliver a joint fringe event may have its attractions for your organisation. Apart from helping to keep costs down, it will also demonstrate to the policy makers that your organisation has support for the issues it is raising, and is taking an integrated approach.

Networking opportunities

The party conferences will provide your organisation with numerous networking opportunities. With sound planning, combined with targeted resourcing and a little bit of luck, the outcomes of attending party conferences can potentially be very rewarding. These are opportunities to develop your existing ties with Scottish Government Ministers, MSPs, councillors, MPs, Peers and other key party activists, and to develop new links with other policy makers whom you want to engage with going forward. The potential outcomes of reinforcing existing links and/or developing new links can, from experience, include persuading a Minister or an MSP to visit a project or business, putting councillors in touch with senior colleagues to discuss ways in which the former can support funding for a local project deemed to be at risk or to consider a regulatory matter. Other outcomes include getting an opportunity to speak to Scottish Government Ministers about concerns, and persuading MSPs to use your briefings for a debate. Conferences will also provide you with an opportunity to speak to MSPs about lodging amendments on your behalf to a specific piece of legislation, or to MPs to do the same with regard to a piece of legislation in the UK Parliament, which is likely to impact upon Scotland.

At the party conference, apart from using your organisation's own stall or fringe event for networking, there are plenty of other networking opportunities which should not be overlooked. The conference programme will feature dozens of fringe events at lunchtime, and evening receptions, and you should use these opportunities to engage with the key policy makers. In addition, there are also formal receptions such as civic receptions often held by the hosting local authority, and the leaders of the political party hosting the conference will also usually hold an evening reception. These will be attended by Scottish Government Ministers, opposition parties' leaders and key spokespersons, MSPs, local councillors and by other party activists as appropriate, and will present your organisation with further opportunities to engage with key politicians. Do not overlook these opportunities, as attending can produce dividends, particularly if you get a chance to engage with those politicians who were on your target list, but who did not attend your fringe event or drop by your stall. However, no matter how informal the event may feel, you are still there to represent your organisation, so be careful about the amount of alcohol you drink, especially when it is being served without charge at a reception.

Follow up action

The mark of a successful conference for any organisation can usually be measured in the quality and number of contacts and action points you have to follow up afterwards, both with key policy makers and with other organisations. The main thing is that your organisation does follow up, and agrees a post conference strategy on how best to progress these contacts and action points. The important thing is to follow up the contacts and action points quickly before the politicians move on to other priorities and issues. If, for example, a Minister or MSP expressed an interest in meeting senior members of your organisation to discuss an issue or to visit one of your businesses or projects, make sure you get the invite letter out quickly, while the politician's memory of meeting your organisation is fresh and positive. Similarly, if the MSP wanted a briefing for a debate in the Scottish Parliament in the week after returning from their party's conference, make sure they get it.

The follow-up action is where, potentially, the costs of paying for your organisation's presence at a conference, will pay for itself. Capitalising on the follow-up action should be an essential part of your organisation's public affairs strategy. It will also help to demonstrate the value of attending these conferences to anyone in your organisation who might be sceptical about the political/practical return. Your follow-up strategy can potentially assist your organisation to take its public affairs strategy to another level, and to make the most of new opportunities for your organisation arising from the conference.

Top Tip 17
The political parties' conferences offer a major platform on which to engage with a wide range of policy makers. Ensure your organisation has a clear post-conference strategy to maximise the benefits of attending to your organisation through follow-up action with key policy makers.

18

Partnership Working

One of the recurring themes referred to in previous chapters is the need to consider whether or not there are opportunities for your organisation to progress specific public affairs activities, or aspects of your overarching public affairs strategy, through partnership working with other organisations. The case and opportunities, for partnership working will be significantly increased if one of the political parties has an overall majority in the Scottish Parliament. Admittedly, there could be reasons why working in partnership might not appeal to your organisation. These could include, for example, the loss of independence and freedom to act, and the need for partners to sign off on specific decisions or actions leading to a slower speed of response. This factor could be particularly damaging if your organisation and its partners are in a fast moving public affairs situation or environment, where the need to respond to events and developments is time critical.

However, operating without allies may mean that you organisation is left to face any storms or political controversy generated by your campaigning alone. This lack of cover and support means that your organisation should not automatically ignore the potential of working with other organisations to secure tangible outcomes for your public affairs activities and strategy. This chapter looks at some of the areas in which partnership working could actually pay dividends for your organisation.

Types of partnership working

If partnership working is a realistic, and an attractive, option for your organisation, you need to give careful consideration to the specific organisations, and to the type of organisations, you want to work with. This will, ultimately, depend upon the issues and policy areas which your organisation is seeking to engage policy makers on, and on the type of organisations which share those interests. Partnership working throws up a number of options.

You could, for example, support the public affairs activities being undertaken by relevant umbrella organisations on behalf of their members, including your own organisation. In this context, how active your support is for such activities will often increase the likelihood that the umbrella organisation will give your organisation some profile on the issues which it is campaigning on. This could be reflected, for example, in your organisation being referred to in the umbrella body's briefing for a debate in the Scottish Parliament, with the briefing then circulated widely to relevant Ministers and to MSPs. Similarly, your organisation might be included in any news releases issued by the umbrella organisation before the debate, possibly including a supporting quote from your organisation's chief executive.

Other options would include working thorough existing networks, both formal and informal, and to support any joint initiatives which have emerged through these channels. Examples include the network of policy officers in the children's sector who meet regularly, both on a formal and on an informal basis, and the children's sector networks engaging with the Scottish Parliament's Cross-Party Group on Children and Young People. With this option it might be the case that another organisation has launched the initiative, with other organisations then getting behind it to lend their support. This could be particularly attractive if the initiative focuses on issues which your organisation feels very strongly about, but lacks the capacity and expertise which would enable it to take the lead, campaigning role.

Signing up to such initiatives will give you a public profile on the issues without generally having to commit large amounts of time and resources. The organisations leading these alliances will naturally want to take the lead role in any face-to-face engagement with Scottish Ministers and other policy makers, and in any related media activities around the campaign. Your organisation's position within the sector, and its level of activity within this particular alliance, could, therefore, have a direct bearing on the extent to which you are included in such engagement and in any media activity undertaken by the lead organisation.

Another option would be for your organisation to seize the initiative, and to lead an alliance of like minded organisations on specific issues. This can be illustrated by the policy and public affairs campaign which Action for Children Scotland led with Barnardo's Scotland, Aberlour, Children 1st and Quarriers on the Scottish Government's Children's Hearings legislation. This campaign secured major changes to the legislation in the Scottish Parliament which, as a result, strengthened children's rights within the legislation. The campaign also won Public Affairs News' 2011 Campaign of the Year under the Devolved Administrations category.

Your organisation's ability to lead such an alliance will depend upon a number of factors, including the level of capacity and experience at its disposal. In addition leading an alliance of organisations will depend upon your organisation's standing, influence and expertise in the policy areas in which the organisations are seeking to campaign. Your organisation's overall status, including its track record on service delivery, will also be significant. This will give your organisation a certain 'authority' to seize the initiative, and for other organisations to be more inclined to support your public affairs aims and objectives by signing up to support your activities or campaign.

If your organisation decides to go down this route, you should try and get as many organisations to sign up as possible. You want to demonstrate to the Scottish Government, to the Opposition parties and to MSPs of all parties, that the specific aims and objectives of your campaign have significant support across the sector or sectors in which your organisation operates. Securing such support will make Scottish Ministers more likely to engage with you, and to respond positively to your policy 'asks'. It will also help to persuade Ministers to look at your proposals seriously, and in detail. For organisations which find that such an approach fails to work, it is advised that you then try the Opposition parties. If, however, your organisation finds itself in a situation where a political party has an overall majority in the Scottish Parliament, and what you are asking for will, ultimately, depend upon a vote in the Scottish Parliament, then mathematically you are unlikely to succeed while that party has a majority, if you choose to rely exclusively on the opposition parties. Success, in these circumstances, will often depend upon your organisation's ability to get the governing party's backbenchers on board, and upon their willingness to work on a cross-party basis to progress the key issues.

Against this background, a more productive path might be, and this will depend upon the issues you are raising, to approach a backbencher from the governing party. You should choose the MSP carefully – either your local MSP, or an MSP with whom you have strong links or an MSP who has a proven track record on the issues you are seeking to raise with the Scottish Government. You need to engage early with this MSP, persuade them of the merits of your case and give them the background brief which they can then use in any discussions with the relevant Scottish Minister. It may be that the MSP will seek to involve representatives from your own organisation, and from your partner organisations, in these discussions. Ideally, you are looking for the MSP to use engagement with the Minister to win approval for the policy proposals you are raising, or for the Minister to make some sort of concession to address your concerns.

A partnership response to legislation

There are a wide range of public affairs activities which could benefit from a partnership approach. One of the most potentially fruitful areas for partnership working is responding to a Bill in the Scottish Parliament. A recommended approach would be to identify issues about the Bill which are of concern/interest to your organisation, and where there is a chance of generating cross-party support, especially in a committee without a government majority, and to then draft suitable amendments. With your amendments drafted, and an MSP sponsor identified and willing to lodge the amendments on your behalf, you should then try and maximise the number of organisations willing to support the amendments.

The more organisations you can get on board the better. This will demonstrate to Scottish Ministers, to the Opposition parties, and to individual MSPs the breadth of support for your amendments. This is vital if your organisation is to generate cross-party support for your amendments, and to increase the chances of the Scottish Government being willing to accept the amendments, or the Opposition parties winning Divisions on the amendments, either at Stage 2 or Stage 3 of the legislation in the Scottish Parliament.

Other partnership activities

Briefing MSPs for a debate in the Scottish Parliament would also lend itself well to a partnership approach. Debates often attract a wide range of interest from organisations, and MSPs can sometimes be swamped by briefing materials from a bewildering array of organisations seeking to brief MSPs for the debate. Receiving a joint briefing which has the support of a number of different organisations will send a powerful message to the Scottish Government, to the Opposition parties and to MSPs of all parties. It will highlight that your organisation is raising issues of substance, which have attracted a good level of support across the sector or sectors in which it operates. The strength of that message will be reinforced by the number of organisations which sign up to support the briefing. Apart from targeting the Minister, you should also contact all of the Opposition parties' relevant spokespersons to update them about your briefing, and to try and build up a cross-party alliance of MSPs behind the issues you are raising.

If your organisation's own attempts to secure a meeting, and/or to raise concerns, with a particular Scottish Minister have proved unsuccessful, you might want to try a different tack. In these circumstances, it is advised that you secure support from like-minded organisations, and send a joint request to the Minister for a meeting, or a joint letter outlining your concerns. Indeed, it might be that this is the direction you choose to take from the outset. With joint requests it is recommended that your organisation takes the initiative. This would generally involve drafting a letter to go to the Minister from your Chief Executive, and circulating the letter to get other organisations to sign up in support. Their names and logos can then be added to the letter to add weight to the request.

To maximise the number of organisations coming on board, it is further recommended that you highlight a limited number of issues in the letter, and in the agenda for the proposed meeting with the Minister. This will provide a focus for the meeting, and will encourage more organisations to confirm their support. Receiving a joint request for a meeting might also prove more attractive to the Minister because it will give them an opportunity to meet, in one meeting, many of the key players in the sector on a particular issue, rather than having to meet all of the main organisations separately, which could be time consuming and counter productive. You might also want to take a

similar, joint approach to meet the relevant spokespersons for each
of the Opposition parties.

Where you are raising concerns with the Scottish Government,
and with the Opposition parties, through a joint letter, it is strongly
recommended that you give consideration to linking this up with some
media activity. Ensuring that your letter receives some coverage in
the media could increase the pressure on the policy makers to address
your collective concerns. That said, your organisation and its partners
must recognise that this is a fine balancing act, because issuing a news
release in support of your joint letter could alienate the policy makers,
and provoke them into responding negatively to your letter. A lot will
also depend upon the issues you are raising, and the implications for the
Scottish Government and for the Opposition parties. In this situation
it is advised that you take soundings from your partner organisations,
and reach a collective view on whether or not to tie in some media
activity (at this stage) to support your letter.

Partnership events

A number of organisations in, for example, the community and
voluntary sector have clubbed together over the years to hold joint
fringe events at political parties' conferences. The appeal of these joint
initiatives has increased with the mounting financial pressure which
many organisations across different sectors have been under due to
economic recession and falling income. Joint fringe events can be an
excellent, cost effective way of raising your organisation's profile on
key issues, while keeping down costs. The challenge with such events
is to ensure that all of the partners work in a collegiate fashion, and
that all the organisations feel that they have benefited equally from
the profile of such events.

Holding a joint parliamentary event with partners is another good
way of maximising your organisation's impact in certain policy
areas. It is important to stress, however, that, in addition to saving on
costs, holding a joint parliamentary event could have specific tactical
advantages. A joint event, with a number of supporting partners,
focusing on certain key issues will, for example, send out a strong
signal of unity to the policy makers, regardless of any differences
between the supporting organisations (and many are likely to be

direct competitors). Sending a clear message to the policy makers about the level of support of organisations behind certain key issues will be critical, particularly if the event is focusing on lines of amendments to new legislation being considered by the Scottish Parliament.

If your organisation does decide to go down the route of a joint parliamentary event, it will need to work carefully and closely with your partner organisations to ensure that the structure of the event best serves your purpose of influencing the policy makers. In this respect, your organisation will need to manage any tensions with regard to which organisations provide speakers for the event, and take the lead on any media activity. If your organisation can get this right, then it will have a real chance to impress the policy makers with a united front on the key issues, which will increase the chances of your organisation's strategy delivering significant outcomes. Where these tensions prove difficult to manage, you might want to opt for inputs from the Minister, from an MSP with a track record in the policy area in which the event is to focus, and on an input from service users. This approach could help to minimise the risks of intra-organisational 'politics' overshadowing the event. Your organisation and its partners need to demonstrate to the policy makers the depth of support within the sector behind the issues you are raising, and that you are willing to set aside any differences your organisations may have with other organisations to try and achieve the policy outcomes you are collectively looking for.

Your organisations will significantly increase their chances of doing so if they can demonstrate unity on the issues, and avoid the event becoming a platform for a succession of chief executives to 'grandstand' on behalf of their organisations. This is completely unnecessary – the politicians will usually have a sound, general awareness that your organisations are reputable and effective. They would not be at your event if they did not think that this was the case. The politicians will be mainly attending because they want to find out more about your issues and about your concerns. They are there to be convinced, and what better way for that than to demonstrate the support across the sector for the issues you are raising.

Top Tip 18
Careful thought should be given to ways in which your organisation can work in partnership to deliver key parts of its wider public affairs strategy. Partnership working will demonstrate to the policy makers that your organisation has wider support for the issues it is raising, and in certain circumstances will make them more likely to make concessions.

19

Working with the Media

To maximise the impact of your organisation's public affairs strategy, and public affairs activities, it is vital that your organisation works closely with the media. Ensuring that the media highlights your organisation's public affairs campaigns and activities will help to raise its profile with the Scottish Government, opposition parties, MSPs, councillors and other key policy makers, as well as with the general public. Securing this engagement will be particularly important if your organisation is campaigning on specific issues and/or is attempting to shape and influence Scottish Government legislation, or other policy initiatives or strategies.

It should be recognised, however, that there might be some occasions in which your organisation takes the view that, because of the sensitivities of a specific policy issue or because of its ongoing negotiations with the Scottish Government or with a local authority or other stakeholder, it would be best (at this stage) not to seek publicity for its public affairs activities. Indeed, even if the Scottish Government or local authority or other stakeholder makes a significant concession in response to your organisation's public affairs strategy, part of the agreement for the concession could well be that there is no publicity for your organisation, or that any publicity is managed exclusively by the Scottish Government or by the local authority or other stakeholder as appropriate. The key thing is that, as part of your organisation's public affairs strategy, you include undertaking a complete risk assessment of how any publicity for your organisation's public affairs activities could impact upon key partners or other stakeholders. For the purpose of this chapter it is assumed that your organisation will want to fully publicise its public affairs activities.

This chapter also relates solely to the use of media for public affairs purposes – your organisation will need to identify how this kind of activity will form part of a wider approach to working with the media.

Taking an integrated approach

The best way for your organisation to ensure that it is able to maximise the level of publicity for its public affairs campaign and/or activities is to take an integrated approach to engaging with key policy makers. Depending upon the size of your organisation, you may wish to seek to establish (if you have not already done so) an external affairs committee which meets regularly to scan the external environment, to identify threats as well as opportunities for your organisation to raise the profile of its work and to engage with senior policy makers. The aim of this committee should be to maximise opportunities for your organisation, and to minimise or manage risks. The committee should play a strategic role within your organisation, particularly in areas such as the development of its public affairs strategy and its media engagement strategy.

It is recommended that such a committee should involve a member of your organisation's senior management team, and the lead officers within your organisation with responsibility for your organisation's services, for policy, for public affairs, for marketing, for media and for internal communications. Community and voluntary organisations would also want to ensure their lead officer for fundraising is involved in the committee. Pitching the representation on this committee at a strategic level within your organisation will help to ensure that the committee, not only acts as a high level information exchange, but also takes decisions which will enable your organisation to capitalise on opportunities to raise its profile and to influence key policy makers, and also to respond early to threats or reputational risks. For smaller organisations, it may be necessary to adapt this model to fit their circumstances, and to take into account issues around capacity and resources.

Regardless of which type of model of approach your organisation takes in these areas, the main thing is that it takes an integrated approach, and that your organisation's lead officers for public affairs and media work closely together to maximise your organisation's ability to capitalise on opportunities to raise its profile, and to engage with senior policy makers. Their success will also depend upon the extent to which they have internal support from within your organisation, and in particular from the senior management team. This type of approach will be essential if your organisation is to enjoy a high profile, and is to influence key policy makers in the Scottish Government and in the Scottish Parliament, and at local government level.

Key aims

One of the first issues which your organisation must address in taking forward public affairs and media activities will be to decide the aims and objectives of such activities. Is your organisation, for example, simply seeking to raise its profile with key policy makers, with the media, with major stakeholders and with the general public? Or is it trying to influence high profile policy debates, or to help shape specific legislation in the Scottish Parliament or policy initiatives and strategies being developed by the Scottish Government or by the Opposition parties or by local authorities? In this respect, your organisation must also develop its key messages, and its main 'political asks', i.e. what action does it want the policy makers to take? Addressing these issues will help to ensure that the public affairs and media activities taken forward by your organisation have a strong focus.

Use of news releases

Many of the public affairs activities undertaken by your organisation are ones which could be supported by a news release to encourage the media to publicise the activities, and to raise your organisation's profile. It will also help to build up support within the Scottish Government, amongst MSPs and within the local government community for any specific policy 'asks' your organisation is making. The success of these news releases, however, will vary, and would depend to a large degree upon what your organisation is seeking to publicise, the subject matter and its general newsworthiness.

Another factor will be the news stories and articles with which your organisation's news release will be competing on a particular day. In this respect, your organisation should try as much as possible, and as far as practicable, to scan the media horizon to see if there are any obvious big news stories which are likely to prevent your organisation getting any publicity through its news releases if issued at the same time. Examples would include the UK Government or the Scottish Government setting their budgets, or other major events, such as elections or party conferences, likely to dominate the media on those particular days.

For an organisation to put out a news release on the same day as these developments would rarely succeed, unless of course the news release relates to issues around, for example, the respective governments' budgets. This could potentially improve the likelihood that your news release will generate publicity for your organisation, but this is still no guarantee of success. Sometimes, even scanning the horizon with the greatest diligence will fail to secure any coverage for your organisation. There is also the risk that some international or national development will dominate the media so completely on a particular day that any news release issued by organisations on the same day will simply vanish without trace. Against this background, the best that organisations can do is to try and minimise the risks that their news release will fail to generate any coverage by avoiding some of the more obvious clashes such as, for example, UK Government or Scottish Government budget days.

News releases can be used to support, and publicise, a wide range of public affairs activities. Examples include issuing a news release to generate publicity for issues your organisation has briefed MSPs on for a key debate in the Scottish Parliament. If your organisation has taken a targeted approach to the debate, and has only briefed a few MSPs, you might want to consider working with one of the MSPs to try and get some national media coverage, or to at least to ensure that the debate, and the MSP's support for your organisation, is featured in the local media within the MSP's constituency or region as appropriate, as well as on social media. In this respect, it is worth bearing in mind that local media is often well supported, with many local newspapers having a significant circulation.

News releases in support of motions lodged by MSPs on behalf of your organisation and its work will also offer useful opportunities to raise your organisation's profile with key policy makers and with the public, and to increase support for any political 'asks' which your organisation raises with the Scottish Government or with other policy makers. Some motions attract significant support from amongst MSPs, and both Action for Children Scotland and Barnardo's Scotland have previously attracted support from over 80 MSPs for motions in support of their work. When it is taken into account that Scottish Ministers will not sign up to motions it can be seen that this is a significant number of MSPs. The opportunities for publicising this specific type of public affairs initiative should, therefore, not be overlooked. An important consideration, however, for your organisation will be to work closely with the sponsoring MSP to liaise on how best to maximise media opportunities.

Your organisation should also consider issuing a news release to highlight its position on legislation going through the Scottish Parliament, especially if an MSP has lodged amendments to the legislation on its behalf. This will help your organisation to try and secure support for its policy position from the Scottish Government, the opposition parties, MSPs, other organisations and from the general public. Consideration should also be given to issuing a news release where your organisation submits evidence to a Scottish Parliament inquiry. Indeed, there have been occasions when organisations have been able to generate greater levels of publicity for the issues raised in their evidence at the point when they submit this evidence, than the parliamentary committee has been able to secure for its final inquiry report.

Media activity should also be undertaken to support any petitions which your organisation has submitted to the Scottish Parliament's Public Petitions Committee. Generating publicity will be particularly important where the petition is focusing on specific policy 'asks'. In this context, your organisation will need to ensure that media activity is a key part of its public affairs campaign in support of the petition. This will have a number of benefits. It will help to raise awareness within the Scottish Government, the opposition parties, amongst MSPs and with other key policy makers, as well as with the general public about your organisation's petition and the policy 'asks' it is making. This will be particularly important in generating support for the petition from the MSP members of the Public Petitions Committee who will be the MSPs deciding on what action should be taken by the Scottish Parliament in response to your organisation's petition. Securing good levels of publicity for the petition could, therefore, prove decisive in securing a positive response from the committee.

News releases should also be issued to support public affairs events. The type of media coverage your organisation aims for will depend upon the nature of the event, and the issues on which the event is focusing. If it is a parliamentary event highlighting major issues, your organisation is more likely to secure national media coverage. By contrast, if the event is with your organisation's local MSP at one of your businesses or services within their constituency, the focus would usually be on the local media, unless the event is contributing to newsworthy, high profile public policy debates. Both these types of events can provide invaluable publicity for your organisation, and make significant, strategic contributions to its work, and to its public affairs campaigns and activities. The success of the event, and of the media coverage generated by the event, will depend upon the aims of the event, and the extent to which your organisation was successful in achieving its objectives and in engaging with key target audiences.

Exclusivity

One issue which your organisation will need to decide in its approach to media coverage in support of its public affairs activities is whether or not to work exclusively with one television or radio broadcaster, or with one newspaper, on a particular news release. An approach based on exclusivity, or on a more general engagement with the media through for example issuing a news release to the Press Association, can both offer advantages and disadvantages. In this context, granting exclusivity to a high profile television or radio broadcaster, or newspaper, would generally guarantee your organisation a good level of media coverage from the media provider. You might consider this if you are planning public affairs activities around, for example, a specialist research report which your organisation is launching, and wanted the report to be considered on an in-depth basis. It would be less effective if your organisation is holding a high profile public affairs event such as, for example, an event for one of your businesses or services to celebrate a landmark anniversary, and for which it is seeking to maximise media coverage.

The general disadvantage of granting exclusivity is that it might mean it proves more difficult for your organisation to extend the level of media coverage for its public affairs activities beyond that provided by your organisation's media partner. This is likely to be because rival media providers may be unwilling to provide coverage when they know that your organisation has an exclusive arrangement with one of their rivals. Against this background, your organisation will need to take a view on which approach is best suited to meet its specific needs and aims in relation to a specific public affairs campaign or public affairs activities.

Media briefings

Your organisation can also try and increase the level of media coverage it secures for its public affairs activities by providing regular briefings to the media. It can do so by ensuring it has regular contacts with those journalists focusing on the policy areas and issues most relevant to your organisation. This will provide your organisation with opportunities to brief the journalists about its public affairs activities and initiatives. By doing so, your organisation will be able to generate interest in planned activities and initiatives. Apart from regular phone and e-mail contacts to cultivate your organisation's ties with journalists, your organisation should also give thought to holding briefing meetings with individual journalists, or with groups of journalists, at which senior members of your organisation can start to explore ideas for stories or features which relate to key aspects of your public affairs activities.

Cultivating ties with the media to support your organisation's public affairs activities, and to raise the profile of your organisation, are important both for national organisations, and for local, community based organisations. Media coverage will play an important role in your organisation's public affairs campaign, and should not be neglected. In this respect, securing publicity for your organisation's public affairs activities will help to build up support for the policy issues upon which your organisation is campaigning. This, in turn, will support your organisation to ensure it helps to shape and influence key public policy debates, and to contribute to legislation, policy initiatives and strategies.

Briefing the media will also deliver significant benefits for local, community based organisations. Using regular briefings to build up your organisation's relationships with journalists will help to ensure that the local media is aware of your organisation, and its work in the local community. Developing close ties in this area will raise the profile of your organisation, and make journalists more likely to regularly feature your organisation in media articles and in their general coverage of events and developments within the local area. Such coverage can potentially play a critical role in strengthening the profile of your organisation within the local community, which could offer important spin-offs in promoting your organisation and its interests. Where, for example, an organisation delivers services on behalf of the local authority raising its profile through these means could help to safeguard future funding and contracts.

Accessibility

Another way in which your organisation will be able to develop its links with the media is to ensure that it maintains appropriate levels of accessibility, and deals efficiently and effectively with media enquiries. By building up your organisation's relationships with the media you will, for example, often find that your organisation is approached for responses and quotes to a wide range of policy issues by journalists working to strict deadlines. This requires your organisation to strike a balance between being accommodating to the journalist to help strengthen your ties with the media, and providing a thoughtful, strategic response which will benefit your organisation, and not damage its reputation.

After all, some of these approaches could potentially steer your organisation into controversial waters unless handled appropriately, and you need to remain mindful of that fact. There is also the danger that your organisation, by providing organisational responses to all such approaches, will earn the reputation of being a 'rent-a-quote' organisation. This could harm your organisation's reputation, and also increases the risks that your organisation will, by providing a response, get sucked into wider controversies, which could be both damaging and embarrassing. This trend was frequently evident during the Independence Referendum campaign, when a number of organisations across different sectors got themselves into challenging situations by endorsing the policy positions of either the Yes or No campaigns when it would appear they had no internal authority to do so. Others came unstuck when they were persuaded to respond to future and/or hypothetical situations presented by a Yes or No vote, and found their answers exploited by both camps for very different purposes. The net result was that they found themselves embroiled in controversies, which led to internal debates about accountability and governance for some of those organisations.

The secret is to ensure that all such approaches are channelled through your organisation's media officer and/or through a senior manager, and that responses to such approaches are all rigorously risk assessed. In this respect, where your organisation is contacted to provide a response to a policy development or issue, before providing such a response you need to consider if it is something which affects your organisation. Other factors would include whether or not it is something upon which your organisation has/should have a corporate view. Your organisation should also consider if providing a response could have an adverse impact upon its relationships with key partners, members or with other stakeholders. Where it is agreed that a response should be made it is important that the response is measured, and is based upon your organisation's experience, evidence base and best practice as appropriate.

If your organisation has robust systems and procedures in place for dealing with media approaches, this area can help your organisation to develop its links with the media, and to raise your organisation's profile. The secret is to ensure that this whole process is overseen by someone within your organisation who is senior enough to take a strategic overview, and has the experience to weigh up the advantages and disadvantages of responding to such approaches, and to determine the manner of your organisation's responses. By following this guidance your organisation can use these approaches to support its public affairs activities effectively, and to raise the profile of your organisation and its work.

Top Tip 19
Maximise publicity for your organisation's public affairs campaign or public affairs activities by taking an integrated, whole organisation approach to engaging with key policy makers supported by appropriate media activities.

20

Online Communications

What do we mean by online communications and social media?

Social media includes a wide range of digital communications technology which has the potential to displace traditional ways of working for campaigning and lobbying work. Traditional media is pretty much a one way street. If your organisation, for example, gets an article printed in a national or local newspaper focusing on its campaign, any key policy makers, organisations or individuals wishing to respond will only have a limited right of reply, or opportunity, to contribute to the policy debate, and may have to be content with a letter or article in the next day's paper which has only a minor impact. That said, securing coverage in itself may, for many organisations, be a significant end in itself. Indeed, the importance of traditional media in securing media coverage which promotes debates, and results in policy makers introducing changes as a result, should not be ignored. In this respect, it is important that your organisation recognises that the use of traditional media and social media are not mutually exclusive, and takes an integrated approach in which both forms of media are used appropriately in your public affairs work.

The big contrast between traditional forms of media work and a social media strategy is that social media is by its very nature interactive, and can therefore be a two-way and/or multi-dimensional process. Response times are also very different. Using social media effectively will allow your organisation to communicate in real time with a wide range of policy makers. Social media can allow small groups of people to directly interact with or influence the activities or policies of the Scottish Government, of local government, of the political parties, of individual MSPs and of other key policy makers. Significantly, it will also allow policy makers and members of the public to communicate directly and publicly with your organisation. As digital technology has evolved, the ability to respond to policy issues and developments has increased exponentially from the confines of fairly static websites to the 'Twittersphere' where responses are now expected in a matter of minutes.

Therefore the most important thing to understand about online communication and about the use of social media, in the context of public affairs, is that it generally represents a faster and more direct way to communicate the messages your organisation is trying to disseminate. It is tempting to treat the use of social media as being absolutely distinct from all other elements of your organisation's influencing work. However, it is wiser to view the use of social media as part of your organisation's overall communications strategy, albeit one with its own special characteristics.

One factor to bear in mind, before looking at the different types of social media, is that the lines of communication between key policy makers and organisations in Scotland is often much shorter than at a UK-level. If, for example, your organisation Tweets about a Cabinet Secretary or MSP you might find that they personally Tweet back, which underlines the need to ensure that your organisation has given careful thought to the messages it wishes to get across to policy makers, to the public and to other target audiences as appropriate.

Types of social media

Twitter: The use of Twitter will potentially enable your organisation to communicate with a wide range of groups, organisations and individuals. Significantly, most politicians at Scottish Government, Scottish Parliament and local government levels, now have Twitter accounts. Tweeting will, therefore, potentially present your organisation with opportunities to get its message across in a simple, direct and succinct way to key audiences, including the Scottish Government and opposition parties, MSPs, journalists and other opinion formers.

In certain circumstances your organisation's Tweet could go 'viral', i.e. be re-Tweeted rapidly and widely beyond the confines of the organisation's usual followers. This can be particularly helpful to your organisation when it has launched a major public affairs campaign, and is seeking to increase levels of support for its key messages and policy 'asks'.

The reverse side of the coin is that your organisation's mistakes can also go viral. In this respect, if your organisation has communicated the wrong message to the wrong person at the wrong time it could find itself the object of unwanted attention across Twitter.

It is important to bear in mind, however, that there are only a limited number of Twitter users in Scotland, with some estimates suggesting a maximum of 10% of the adult population of Scotland are active Twitter users.

If, however, your organisation does decide to start Tweeting, it should first recognise that the speed of Twitter requires 24 hour engagement. This brings its own challenges. The ill-judged Tweet, for example, that your organisation sends out at 5pm could be re-Tweeted exponentially, to the extent that by 9am the following morning your organisation has been widely mocked or criticised across Twitter.

Facebook: By contrast, the use of Facebook will, for many organisations, be a much more familiar form of social media. In this respect, your organisation's Facebook strategy should look similar to its general web strategy. Facebook is less interactive than Twitter and while other users can leave comments on your organisation's Facebook page, they can be deleted by the moderators of the page.

Although requiring less constant updating than Twitter, your organisation's Facebook pages will still require new material regularly. This is to ensure that the content remains informative, and continues to be relevant, and of interest, to key policy makers. One of the advantages of Facebook in supporting public affairs campaigns and activities is that it can encourage and promote discussion, that will be much deeper and more substantive than exchanges on Twitter which are subject to 140 character limits.

Facebook users who like your page will have your updates posted on their timelines, so they will be automatically informed about new activity. Some organisations produce a steady stream of pictures and headlines designed purely to get existing contacts to share a link to encourage more users to like their page. There is a danger that overuse of this kind of 'click-bait' material can makes your organisation look ridiculous.

The impact of your organisation's Facebook activity will, however, depend upon the extent to which your organisation has the capacity and staff to contribute to and support your Facebook pages. Ensuring your organisation has sufficient capacity and resources will be particularly important in providing prompt responses to policy discussions and debates on your organisation's Facebook pages. Prompt responses on Facebook will be essential if your organisation is to ensure that it does not lose any momentum in its Facebook activities, and if these activities are to help to raise the profile of your organisation, and of its public affairs activities. Responding quickly on Facebook will also enable your organisation to intervene early in policy discussions and debates which, without such interventions, could prove unhelpful to your organisation's public affairs campaign or activities and, in the worst case scenario, potentially derail its public affairs campaign or activities, and cause lasting reputational damage.

Websites: The use of websites is generally the least interactive element of the social media universe. This makes it the easiest part of social media to control. An organisation's website is often a key source of information about the organisation for MSPs, local councillors and other key policy makers, as well as to the general public. It is, therefore, crucial that your organisation ensures its website is informative, attractive, and is regularly updated. A good way to do this may be to use a campaign blog as a central feature of the website, consisting of regular news and updates on the progress you are making.

Where your organisation is undertaking a specific public affairs campaign or activities, your website will provide significant opportunities to raise the profile of the campaign/activities. The website will enable your organisation to publicise the campaign/activities, and to get across its key messages and policy 'asks' to a wide range of policy makers, as well as to the general public. Providing regular updates on the website will help your organisation to reach a larger audience, and to potentialy gain greater support for its key messages and policy 'asks'.

Twitter and Facebook posts can also link to your website, and encourage people to see the information there. However material on your website that people disagree with can also be easily shared via Twitter and Facebook – so a website needs to be part of a wider social media strategy.

Uses of social media

Social media can be a useful tool in public affairs work. It is important to remember, however, that it is not the only tool available to your organisation, and that it will not always be the best or most appropriate tool to use in particular circumstances. If, for example, your organisation wants to thank a Scottish Government Minister or MSP or local councillor in real time for an intervention on behalf of your organisation, or on behalf of those your organisation works for, then social media will enable your organisation to do so quickly, and in a very public, wide-reaching forum. The same consideration would apply if your organisation wants to challenge a policy maker about their policy position/actions. Facebook would be particularly helpful where you are seeking to build up a community of support for your policy position and/or public affairs campaign.

Limitations

The risk for your organisation of relying too heavily on Twitter, Facebook or on other types of social media is that this approach could exclude some groups of potential supporters from backing your organisation's work and public affairs campaign. Your organisation should take this into account when developing its public affairs strategy, especially if engaging with the general public is a key part of this strategy.

The impact of your organisation's social media activities for the purpose of public affairs work and campaigning will also be limited if you undertake these activities in isolation. It is essential that your organisation takes an integrated approach, and that its social media activities support and form an important part of its public affairs activities. Getting the political approach right will ensure that your organisation's campaign delivers tangible outcomes.

To take an example, a recent health campaign focused on a range of imaginative activities to raise awareness of the risks posed by a certain illness. The campaign used both traditional and social media, and it secured widespread national media coverage as well as sustained social media attention.

While the aim of the campaign might just have been to raise awareness of the illness for a day, in which case it appears to have accomplished its mission, questions remain about whether or not such awareness raising campaigns deliver effective, long term outcomes.

To put this in perspective, the campaign activities took place during a parliamentary recess, and do not appear to have involved directly influencing politicians. Some of the activities suggested by the campaign, such as preventative health checks, could have taken place with MSPs inside or near the Scottish Parliament to widen the campaign's impact. The profile of the campaign could also have been further increased by the use of a Members' debate or motion in the Scottish Parliament, both of which would have worked well with the media campaign. If the campaign has used this kind of activity to raise specific policy 'asks' with the Cabinet Secretary, with the aim of securing Government support for these policy 'asks', the campaign could have led to policy changes that resulted in even more lives being saved.

So while the campaign secured a good level of national media for a day, as well as some initial interest on social media, because the objectives of the campaign were limited to media work, with no exploration of potential policy 'asks', the opportunity to integrate these activities with direct lobbying was missed. This could have delivered policy changes to ensure that even more lives were changed for the better. This is a lost opportunity for what was otherwise an excellent, highly imaginative campaign.

Another factor that can limit the effectiveness of the use of social media in public affairs campaigns and activities is the element of uncertainty inherent in social media. This can make it difficult to predict the likely impact of your organisation's intervention through social media. Sometimes campaign messages you hope will go viral do not hit that level of engagement, while messages you anticipate will have a more limited impact circulate widely. The main thing for your organisation is to ensure that it factors in this element of uncertainty when it is planning social media activities as part of a wider public affairs campaign or intervention.

Key factors in progressing social media activities

Capacity: One of the main factors your organisation will need to address at an early stage in developing its social media activities is what capacity you have to sustain these activities. This is vital because there is nothing worse than an under-resourced social media campaign. Capacity may mean some additional funding, but it will often be the capacity of existing staff – a factor that will be at a premium for many organisations. The goal should be to ensure that your organisation has sufficient capacity to deliver social media activities that are relevant, up-to-date and sufficiently interesting to secure support from key target audiences.

If the focus of your organisation's social media activities is on your website, who will ensure that the website is regularly updated? Alternatively, if your organisation prioritises Facebook, who will act as a moderator, and if your organisation seeks to concentrate on Twitter, who within the organisation will take responsibility for responding to Tweets during out-of-office hours?

Authority: Approaching social media as an 'add-on', and assigning responsibility for your organisation's social media activities to a junior member of staff, will potentially undermine your organisation's ability to use the medium effectively. Your organisation should give responsibility to someone who knows your organisation well, and has sufficient authority to be able to respond to any challenges. As previously discussed, the speed of social media means that response cannot be routinely delayed while responses, including where necessary rebuttal statements, are authorised. This person should also be able to ensure that an integrated approach is taken across your organisation and that the input of key staff helps to inform the content of your organisation's social media activities.

Clear messaging: To maximise the effect of your organisation's social media activities it is vital that you take time to develop key messages for your public affairs campaign or activities. It is recommended that your organisation should also develop social media lines in parallel with the policy 'asks' it is hoping to secure. Having clear messages and policy 'asks' will help your organisation to raise the profile of, and to increase support for, its campaign or public affairs activities.

Need for an integrated approach: It is strongly recommended that your organisation avoids taking a narrow, isolated approach to the use of social media to support its public affairs campaigns and activities. The use of social media should not be seen as an end in itself. Instead social media should be viewed as potentially a very effective tool which can, in conjunction with the use of other activities, be used to progress your organisation's key issues and campaigns. To maximise the effectiveness of your social media activities in this context, it is important, however, to take an integrated approach, in which the use of social media is an important element of your organisation's wider public affairs strategy.

Top Tip 20

Organisations should give careful thought to how the messages they wish to channel through social media to policy makers, to the public and to other target audiences as appropriate relate to the policy objectives sought, rather than view the two elements of public affairs work as separate.

21

Influencing Local Government

The changing local government context

The last few years have seen an unprecedented series of changes to local government in Scotland. In 2007 multiple ring-fenced budgets were replaced with Single Outcome Agreements, which gave much greater financial autonomy to councils. The integration of local authority social care functions with health board responsibilities, discussed later in this chapter, is possibly the most far-reaching public service reform since the establishment of the Scottish Parliament, and has given councilors more influence than ever before. The Community Empowerment (Scotland) Act 2015 created new responsibilities on local authorities to engage with, listen to and respond to communities in their area. Recent years have also seen ever higher budget settlements, and a number of councils leave COSLA to form the Scottish Local Government Partnership. There are continuing debates about local government finance, and how much responsibility central government should have for education.

Against this background, influencing local authorities will sometimes be a much more immediate, and important consideration for certain types of organisation, than seeking to influence Scottish Government Ministers and MSPs. These include organisations such as community and voluntary organisations which are based within local communities, and/or deliver services on behalf of local authorities, and/or rely on the latter for funding, for the use of premises and for other facilities. There are also organisations such as businesses which will have a significant level of engagement with local authorities in areas including, for example, planning, environmental health, health and safety and trading standards. For these organisations it is likely that the key focus of their influencing work will often be on the local authority, and on the local authority's elected members and officers.

Significantly, while the above types of organisation will need to have a strong focus on the local authority for the relevant area, they will also need to monitor the impact of policy initiatives and strategies, and legislation, developed by the Scottish Government. It is, therefore, strongly recommended that such organisations, while focusing their influencing work on the local authorities, must be careful not to neglect establishing and/or maintaining relationships with the Scottish Government and with MSPs. The secret is to develop an integrated approach in which your organisation develops a public affairs strategy which is flexible enough to switch its focus between local and central government as conditions and circumstances require.

Engaging with COSLA

If engaging with the local authority is critical to your organisation's interests and business, it is important that you consider ways in which your organisation can develop its ties with the local authorities' umbrella body COSLA (Convention of Scottish Local Authorities), However, recent years have seen COSLA's role challenged by new bodies, such as the Scottish Local Government Partnership (SLGP), so it is worth your organisation checking what the membership of the respective local authority groupings is as part of its engagement strategy with the local authorities.

If your organisation has regular, high level contact with local authorities through, for example, providing services on their behalf, there could be major advantages in developing strategic ties with COSLA. This, however, will not be appropriate for all organisations, especially those organisations which do not have a national role, and/or only have limited capacity and resources to undertake public affairs activities.

However, COSLA cannot impose decisions on its members where they lack unanimity on particular issues. In this respect, it is worth remembering that the policy initiatives and schemes developed by COSLA are often designed to serve as best practice for member councils, rather than being binding policies to which member councils must strictly adhere.

Despite this, building up and/or maintaining relationships with key COSLA spokespersons and officials can still present advantages for certain types of organisation, particularly large businesses, umbrella organisations and national organisations. The main advantages would include assisting these organisations to strengthen their intelligence gathering around key trends and developments within the local government community, and being recognised by COSLA as a 'preferred partner' in strategic policy areas. Such organisations can strengthen their ties with COSLA by building relationships and developing key contacts amongst COSLA's elected members and officers with lead responsibility for the policy areas in which the organisation is most active or has an interest.

A further way in which organisations can develop their relationship with COSLA is to attend its annual conference. The conference is a high profile gathering of the local government community's political leadership. It is attended by council leaders, councillors and by senior officers, and offers significant networking opportunities for organisations. There are a number of options for organisations to maximise their networking impact at the conference. The conference features an exhibition 'market place' in which various organisations across different sectors can hire exhibition spaces. These spaces can offer useful opportunities to engage with elected members and senior officers. Other options include staging a lunchtime 'fringe' event or seminar, along the lines of the fringe events at the political parties' conferences, on key policy issues which your organisation is seeking to prioritise. Some organisations, on the other hand, prefer to send delegates to COSLA's conference, and to attend the conference's evening reception, both of which can also offer good networking opportunities.

Engagement with individual councils

Some organisations will seek to engage with specific local authorities on the basis that they are based in, or have interests within, the local authority area. In this respect, if your organisation is running a business or services within a particular local authority area you should identify the outcomes you are seeking from engaging with the local authority. Your organisation should also consider the type of opportunities that exist for your organisation to engage with the local authority, and the level at which your organisation's engagement should be targeted.

The level of engagement your organisation needs with a local authority will depend upon the nature of its business, services or interests. If your organisation is seeking to raise its profile you should consider a programme of meetings with the council leader, with the councillors acting as spokespersons in the policy areas prioritised by, or relevant to, your organisation, and with other key councillors to brief them about your organisation's work. You should also seek regular meetings with the council officers, as the latter will have a major role to play in various areas which impact upon your organisation including, for example, planning, the commissioning of services etc.

Apart from meetings, you should also seek to involve your local authority contacts in any events your organisation holds to celebrate its work in the local authority area. This, for example, could be a landmark anniversary for your business, or for one of your organisation's projects or services within the local authority area, or it could be an event to celebrate the success of your organisation. Inviting your key local authority contacts to participate in such events will help to build up/ strengthen your relationship with the local authority. This could be crucial going forward in terms of safeguarding your organisation's interests within the local authority by, for example, securing new contracts or support to maintain your organisation's services, or to develop its business etc.

Please remember that in hosting such events your organisation must remain sensitive to the need to ensure political balance in terms of whom you invite to the event, and the parties and political interests they represent. When your organisation comes to consider compiling the guest list, for example, the first question to address is which of your contacts are the key ones to attract? You must also consider which are the ones you simply cannot afford not to be there, either in terms of inviting them to the event and/or recognising their importance to your organisation by giving them some formal role at the event, e.g. giving the welcoming speech to open the event etc. Careful thought, and risk assessment, must be given to this aspect of the event, as it will have a direct bearing on the outcomes your organisation is able to achieve through the event, including strengthening your organisations' ties with the local authority. If you get this wrong, this could be potentially damaging to your organisation, and could overshadow your future relations with the local authority.

Community planning

Another reason why organisations should consider ensuring that their public affairs strategies include a focus on local authorities is to ensure that they are able to contribute to, and influence, the community planning process in each local authority area. Community planning is the process through which local authorities, health boards and other public bodies plan and provide public services within these areas. Under community planning the community planning partners must consult community bodies and other persons during the community planning process. This potentially offers organisations significant opportunities to influence the community planning process, and the design and delivery of services within the local authority areas in which they operate. Ensuring that your organisation engages with local authorities will potentially help to maximise its impact in the community planning process, and give it an important say in how services are planned and delivered in the local authority area.

New arrangements between local authorities and health boards

Your organisation will also need to be aware, if it is involved in providing health and social care services and/or children's services, of the new structures and frameworks which have been introduced within local authorities, as these will have a bearing on its public affairs strategy. The Public Bodies (Joint Working) (Scotland) legislation was introduced to promote the integration of health and social care, and to deliver closer working between local authorities and health boards. This means that, in terms of public affairs activities, organisations involved in these areas will have to engage with both the local authorities and the health boards, and with the joint structures introduced through the legislation. This could well present your organisation with various new opportunities, but it should also be recognised that there might be challenges involved in developing the most effective and efficient ways of devising public affairs strategies to engage with the new joint local authority/health board arrangements and structures introduced by the legislation. In any event, if your organisation is involved in health and social care in these new structures should not be ignored.

Third sector interfaces

Every local authority area in Scotland has a Third Sector Interface (TSI), which aims to support local voluntary and community groups. They are known by a variety of names, reflecting their diverse history and heritage, including Volunteer Centre, Centre for Voluntary Service or Social Enterprise Network, local Voluntary Action agency or even just as the TSI. Whatever they are called, they can be an invaluable resource for advice and support in engaging with local political structures. Recent legislation, such as the Public Bodies (Joint Working) Act 2014 has given TSIs an important function in representing the local voluntary sector, for example on Integrated Joint Boards. Membership of TSIs is relatively inexpensive, and may well be an excellent investment. The TSIs are all independent and autonomous, and can have quite different structures depending on the local context, which can make relating to them complex for national organisations with local branches. However, building a relationship with local TSI structures can be an important element of your local public affairs strategy.

> **Top Tip 21**
> Develop a public affairs strategy which is flexible enough to switch its focus between local and national government as your organisation's aims and objectives require, and conditions and circumstances dictate.

22

Any other Business

This guide has provided insights into how organisations across different sectors can best influence key policy makers, including Scottish Ministers, the Opposition parties, individual MSPs and senior members of the local government community, to achieve their policy aims and objectives.

Once your organisation has identified the main issues which will form the focus of its public affairs strategy, it needs to then consider the type of activities which will be most likely to maximise the impact of this strategy. Your organisation will know which of the activities outlined in this guide will be the most appropriate to deliver its public affairs strategy, and when it would be most appropriate to undertake these activities. The key is to adapt these activities, and the timing of the different stages and activities within your strategy, to suit the relevant political and policy context.

Above all else, organisations should take a confident approach to their public affairs work. It is important not to forget that organisations across different sectors make an important contribution to our society, and that the Scottish Ministers, opposition parties, individual MSPs and other policy makers are interested in their successes, as well as in the challenges they face. Your organisation should, therefore, approach its public affairs strategy with some optimism that the issues you are raising will be considered on their merit, and with renewed confidence from reading this guide that it has developed and strengthened its existing skills and capacity to deliver a highly successful, cost effective public affairs strategy to achieve its policy aims and objectives.

But as well as thinking about your organisation – its plans and aspirations, strengths and weaknesses, challenges and potential successes – you should also take the time to assess what you plan to do from the point of view of the potential audience. Can you think like a politician? If you were the MSP or councillor that was the target of your public affairs campaign how would you feel about the campaign?

There is a common caricature of politicians as only being in politics for personal aggrandisement. But being a politician can be a fairly thankless task. Doing the job with any kind of diligence means long hours, often with very little actual sense of making a difference. Your organisation's public affairs work, if done well, can therefore offer the politician the chance to make a change – and after all it is the ability to affect change that drew most MSPs and councillors into politics in the first place.

However, if done poorly, public affairs campaigns can add to the frustration of being a politician. Except on rare occasions the politicians you are seeking to lobby will be less knowledgeable than you about the situation you are lobbying them on. Given that politicians are human, and lack access to stores of magic fairy dust, you are therefore more likely to know what needs to be done to solve your problem or address your concern than they are. Therefore if you approach a politician only with a problem, and no suggestion of a solution you are likely to frustrate both yourself and the politician. If you can give the politician something to do, and options to work with, then you are likely to secure some action. If you cannot think of a viable course of action, why should the politician devise a plan for you?

The temptation in this situation is to try to educate the politician to a similar level of knowledge to yourself, in the hope that they will then be able to identify a way forward. In practice this can mean subjecting them to an hour-long exposition on the details of your concern – and after the lecture has finished, a frustrated politician sitting there thinking "but what do you actually want me to DO?". As lobbyist you may leave the meeting pleased that the politician now understands your issues – but you are unlikely to see anything happen as a result of the meeting.

So what should you do if you are stuck for ideas for change, but want to launch a public affairs campaign? Sadly, the only thing to do is wait until you have clear demands and requests. Go back to the beginning of the guide – rethink your plans if necessary – but do not attempt to launch into a piece of work if all you have are problems.

You will need solutions, and finding them mid-campaign will only be more difficult.

But once you have an answer, a call, a demand or proposal for change you can build a public affairs campaign round it, and deliver the change you need.

Bibliography

A curriculum for excellence: The Curriculum Review Group, Scottish Government, November 2004, [www.gov.scot].

About Members' Bills: Scottish Parliament, 5th Edition, Version 1: Scottish Parliament, June 2016, [www.parliament.scot].

Concordat between the Scottish Government and local government: Scottish Government [www.gov.scot].

Devolved and reserved matters explained: Scottish Parliament [www.parliament.scot].

Guidance on Public Bills: Scottish Parliament, Session 5 Edition (Version 1, June 2016), [www.parliament.scot].

How to submit a public petition: Scottish Parliament [www.parliament.scot].

National Performance Framework: Scottish Government, [www.gov.scot].

'Pepper v Hart': Standard Note: SN/PC/392, 22 June 2005, House of Commons Library.

Scotland's Economic Strategy: Scottish Government, March 2015 [www.gov.scot].

Scottish Ministers, Law Officers and Parliamentary Liaison Officers: Session 5, Scottish Parliament [www.parliament.scot].

Scottish Parliament committees – what are they and what do they do?: Scottish Parliament [www.parliament.scot].

Scottish Planning Policy: June 2014, Scottish Government [www.gov.scot].

Smith Commission - Report of the Smith Commission for further devolution of powers to the Scottish Parliament: 27 November 2014.

Standing Orders of the Scottish Parliament: 5th Edition, Scottish Parliament, April 2016, [www.parliament.scot].

The Code of Conduct for Members of the Scottish Parliament, 6th Edition, Revision 1: Scottish Parliament, 8 June 2016, [www.parliament.scot].

'Understanding the Legislative Process': Scottish Parliament [www.parliament.scot].

Index

welsh academic press

SNP

The History of the Scottish National Party

(Second Edition)

'lucid, comprehensive and balanced - an invaluable guide to the SNP"

David Torrance

'There is scholarship on every page. It will become the definitive reference work on the nationalist strand of Scottish politics and Scottish history...the early days in particular are extremely well done, with close attention to original sources...impressive and has never been so well set out before.'

Scottish Affairs

The first full-length history of the Scottish National Party which traces the fortunes of the SNP from its establishment in 1934 to winning power in the Scottish Parliament.

978-1-86057-057-5   319pp   £19.99   PB

welsh academic press

HUGH MACDIARMID
Black, Green, Red and Tartan

'MacDiarmid ... valued honesty and wisdom and would have saluted them in Bob Purdie ... [his book] would also have won MacDiarmid's heart for its pace, its wit, its clarity and its entertainment.'

Owen Dudley Edwards

'Bob Purdie has analysed Hugh MacDiarmid's politics in this important new book. As the sage said, politics is "Bairns' play" compared to poetry - but essential to get right.'

Professor Christopher Harvie

Essential reading for all those with an interest in contemporary Scotland, this is the first study of Hugh MacDiarmid (1892-1978), the most important literary figure of twentieth century Scotland, by a political historian and provides a unique contribution to the understanding of MacDiarmid's politics.

978-1-86057-057-5   157pp   £29.99   HB

welsh academic press

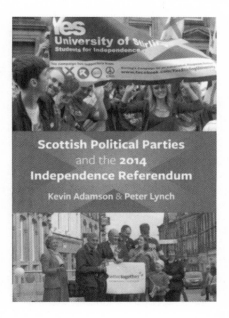

Scottish Political Parties
and the 2014
Independence Referendum

Although the referendum was fought by two umbrella campaign groups - Yes Scotland and Better Together - political parties remained central to the campaign and shaped the nature of the referendum in the Scottish Parliament.

This book analyses the referendum roles and activities of the political parties during the campaign, places the independence referendum in international context through examining other sovereignty referendums and looks at the emergence of new political organisations like Radical Independence and National Collective.

978-1-86057-121-3   172pp   £24.99   PB

welsh academic press

TOMMY SHERIDAN
A Political Biography

'A timely and rigorous biography of Scotland's most flawed politician'

Paul Hutcheon, The Sunday Herald

'This book is an important contribution to understanding the lessons from the wreckage of one of the most fascinating figures of modern Scottish politics.'

Professor James Mitchell, University of Strathclyde

'This is an important story that needs to be told, retold and understood...The rise and fall of Tommy Sheridan and the Scottish Socialist Party is a gripping tale, worthy of fiction, and one which touches on many aspects of Scottish life.'

Gerry Hassan, from the Foreword

978-1-86057-119-0   384pp   £25.00   HB